THE BOOK OF TOPIARY

VIEW IN LEVENS GARDENS: SHOWING GARDENER'S HOUSE

THE BOOK OF TOPIARY

BY

CHARLES H. CURTIS, F.R.H.S.

AND

W. GIBSON

"The man who sneers at me for admiring, as I
do, a well cut peacock, may take my assurance
in advance that I will neither kick him nor
abuse him; but pity him I must."

SHIRLEY HIBBERD

CHARLES E. TUTTLE CO.: PUBLISHERS
Rutland, Vermont & Tokyo, Japan

Representatives

Continental Europe: BOXERBOOKS, INC., *Zurich*

British Isles: PRENTICE-HALL INTERNATIONAL, INC., *London*

Australasia: BOOK WISE (AUSTRALIA) PTY. LTD.
1 Jeanes Street, Beverley 5009, South Australia

*Published by the Charles E. Tuttle Company, Inc.
of Rutland, Vermont & Tokyo, Japan
with editorial offices at
Suido 1-chome, 2–6, Bunkyo-ku, Tokyo, Japan*

© *1985 by Charles E. Tuttle Co., Inc.*

*Library of Congress Catalog Card No. 84-50509
International Standard Book No. 0-8048-1491-0*

First Tuttle edition, 1985

PRINTED IN JAPAN

CONTENTS

LIST OF ILLUSTRATIONS

viii   # LIST OF ILLUSTRATIONS

PUBLISHER'S FOREWORD

TOPIARY has a surprisingly long history, tracing a course
from ancient Greece, through the courtyards of the Roman
empire and the inner castle gardens of medieval Europe, to
the magnificent palace grounds of the seventeenth century.
During this latter period, the art reached its zenith; but, as
with most fashions, it rapidly degenerated into extravagant
excess. The butt of eighteenth century critics, most notably
Addison and Pope, it was assailed as a "monument to
perverted taste."

Whatever one's aesthetic viewpoint, it cannot be denied
that topiary held a powerful spell over horticulture for more
than a hundred and fifty years. It at least lays claim to our
attention as one of the most important influences on Western
landscape gardening. Versailles stands as a splendid example
of its perfection, but its legacy can also be seen in trimly kept
cottage gardens in rural England. There, topiary enthusiasts
diligently shear hedges, shrubs, and trees into shapes and
designs of their fancy. Some translate their skill into simple,
straight-edged privet borders or geometric arches of box;
others unleash their imaginations and pursue globes, pyramids, spirals, and serpentine columns topped by peacocks.

Topiary lies in sharp contrast to the gardening arts of the
East, which seek to humor nature and emulate her form. In
modeling mathematical figures, topiary loves to deviate from
it as much as possible. Despite this gulf, the two approaches
are not completely disparate. Both demand the greatest
discipline, both submit to the rule of time, only achieving

results after many years of labor, and both presume that nature, left to herself, is not an entirely adequate subject of appreciation.

This book, first published in 1904, is reprinted at a time when the art is experiencing a welcome revival. Though some gardeners may balk at topiary's more bizarre examples, few can help but admire the patient genius of its practitioners or fail to be intrigued by its long and involved history. The publisher dares to hope that some readers may even be tempted by the practical sections of the work to take up the scissors themselves.

INTRODUCTION

It is extremely fortunate that the Editor made no limitations, beyond that of space, when giving me the invitation to contribute a historical account of the Art of Topiary, as a sort of preface to the practical advice given in later chapters by Mr Gibson, who has charge of the wonderful collection of clipped trees at Levens Hall. This is fortunate, because it would have been difficult either to wholly praise or wholly blame an art that for at least a century and a half provided English gardens with their outstanding feature. It were easy for us to dismiss the whole subject of Topiary by affecting a great superiority and referring to it only as a monument of perverted taste, but that would neither provide interest nor give instruction, and it is hoped that both these ends may be served so far as the space at disposal will permit.

As it is an undoubted fact that for about one hundred and fifty years Topiary was both fashionable and popular, it follows that, whatever our taste may be, a consideration of the subject cannot be lacking in interest. Never did a horticultural fashion retain its hold upon a gardening public so long as Topiary, but as fashions rarely come spontaneously but are rather arrived at by a kind of evolutionary process, so the art of Verdant Sculpture must have had its Early History, followed by a development of design limited only by the ingenuity of the gardener. Then came what one may call the Golden Age of Topiary, when every garden having any pretensions whatever to importance was more or less notable according to the degree of formality found in its design and furnishing. The inevitable reaction followed next, and had its beginning in a Crusade which found able supporters in those two brilliant essayists and satirists, Addison and Pope. The old order changed, and considering its age, it changed with a rapidity for which there seems to be no parallel in horticulture. No doubt many trees were permitted to grow naturally after years of close cropping and carving, but doubtless also many thousands were uprooted and destroyed by the landscape gardeners who were practising—notably Bridgeman and Kent—when the decline of Topiary set in. And not only were clipped trees destroyed, but many a splendid close trimmed hedge of box and yew was swept away, leaving the garden unsheltered and unsecluded. Extremes met, as was but natural, when once the tide of fashion turned, and it has been left for the present times to properly adjust the balance between extreme formality on the one hand and too close a copy of nature on the other.

We can appreciate the shelter and beauty of a well trimmed hedge in the garden, and, in its proper place, we find no fault with a straight terrace walk. Still further, we are collecting old sundials or fashioning new ones on old models, and in some of the best gardens of the day the garden seats have a comfortable old-time appearance.

The principle of associating like with like is gaining ground, and in numerous fine establishments the interest of the place is wonderfully increased and extended by gardens devoted to certain subjects. We have Rose Gardens, Rhododendron Gardens, Bamboo Gardens, Michaelmas Daisy Gardens, etc., and lastly, we have Topiary Gardens. These latter do not now as heretofore overpower everything else; they are simply part of a whole scheme for providing a continuation of pleasure, beauty and interest; they serve as a reminder

BOX TREE COTTAGE   **RUSTINGTON**

of a quaint stage in the progress of horticulture, and show what a wonderful vitality is possessed by yew, box, and some few other evergreen shrubs.

This little book, then, is not placed before the public with any fervent hope that it will incite garden lovers to at once sally forth with shears and scissors to attack the nearest yew tree; nor is it issued with a desire that garden makers may be induced to plant clipped trees extensively. Further, the "Book of Topiary" can hardly be said to "supply a long felt want" in the general sense in which that very hackneyed phrase is used. Why comes it, then? What are its claims to popular consideration? It comes to provide an hour's reading upon one of the most distinct and interesting branches of horticulture that the art has ever produced. Its claims to consideration are, chiefly, that in it are gathered together the main incidents that go to make up the history of Topiary, and it presents to readers the cultural experience of one whose opportunities for gaining such experience are unequalled.

Topiarian history is somewhat difficult to piece together, and, so far as the writer is aware, no attempt has hitherto been made to place such a history before the gardening public. It is, therefore, modestly suggested that this work is somewhat unique among books dealing with horticultural subjects, and it is hoped it may be found to deserve a position in every garden library.

C. H. CURTIS.

TOPIARY

"If I do not defend the taste through thick and thin, I am prepared
to admit that much may be said in its favour, and it is far from my
intention to denounce it as either extravagant or foolish. It may be
true, as I believe it is, that the natural form of a tree is the most
beautiful possible for that particular tree, but it may happen that we
do not always want the most beautiful form, but one of our own
designing, and expressive of our ingenuity."—*Shirley Hibberd.*

MODERN horticultural works, and especially those that
are of the Dictionary type, do not as a rule take any
notice whatever of Topiary, and those in which it
is noticed deal with the subject with a brevity that is
provoking, inasmuch as the student is little or none
the wiser for the information given. "Johnson's
Gardeners' Dictionary" is silent on the subject, and
"Cassell's Popular Gardening" may be searched in vain
for any reference to it.

Mr G. Nicholson, F.L.S., V.M.H., in his celebrated
"Dictionary of Gardening," writes, under Topiary,
"Although the absurd fashion of cutting and torturing
trees into all sorts of fantastic shapes has, happily,
almost passed away, yet, as the art of the Topiarist was
for a considerable period regarded as the perfection of
gardening, some mention of it is desirable here. When
the fashion first became general in Britain, it is probably
impossible to ascertain; but it reached its highest point
in the sixteenth century, and held its ground until
driven out of the field in the last (eighteenth) century
by the natural or picturesque style. From an archæo-
logical point of view, it is not to be regretted that

4

A PIG CUT IN BOX AT COMPTON WYNYATES

examples of Topiary work on a large scale still exist in several British gardens." Turning to the very recent "Cassell's Dictionary of Gardening" an all too concise account is found, but Mr W. P. Wright admits therein that Topiary "finds favour in many quarters to-day, although it only differs in degree and not in principle from the best examples of the Topiary art of the sixteenth century."

Encyclopædias tell us very little of Topiary, and even that monumental work the "Encyclopædia Britannica" contains within its portly tomes no reference to so historically interesting a subject, unless it be curiously hidden away. And even that very useful work "Chambers's Encyclopædia" passes over Topiary as though such an art never existed.

To students of Etymology the word Topiary itself is of considerable interest. For the present work it must suffice to say that it is derived from the Latin *topiarius*, pertaining to ornamental gardening. One dictionary definition or meaning of the word is "shaped by cutting or clipping" and horticulturists will agree that this definition is both clever and descriptive, for Topiary work consists in giving all kinds of more or less fanciful forms to trees, hedges, and arbours.

An interesting reference is made in the "History of Oxfordshire" to the use of the phrase "Topiary Work." It is stated therein that "at Hampton Court, which was laid out about the middle of the reign of Henry VIII. by Cardinal Wolsey, there was a labyrinth, which still exists, covering only the quarter of an Acre of ground, yet its walks extending by their volutions over nearly half a mile. The walls also were covered with Rosemary. It was also long celebrated for its trees cut into grotesque forms, which Dr Plot admired and dignified with the name of Topiary Works."

EARLY HISTORY

"Little low hedges, round like welts, with some pyramids, I like well; and in some places fair columns, upon frames of carpenters' work."—*Bacon*.

JUST how far back in the history of gardens and gardening the art of Topiary was first practised there is no means of telling, but we know that gardening was first practised as a source of food supply, and that pleasure gardening did not occupy a very prominent position among the arts and sciences until civilisation had made considerable advances. Architecture had progressed in a wonderful manner and reached a high state of perfection long before horticulture assumed any great importance. To use Lord Bacon's elegant words, " when ages grow to civility and elegancy, men come to build stately, sooner than to garden finely, as if gardening were the greater perfection." This being so, it does not seem so very unreasonable to presume that the ancient builders of stately edifices would not in designing the surrounding gardens, plant trees and shrubs likely to mask, soften, or detract in any way from the architectural features created at so great an expenditure of time and money. They would the rather be likely to plant the more formal trees near the mansion, keeping the more graceful at a distance. The love of the formal among the Greeks may be evidenced from the writings of Theocritus, the pastoral poet of Greece, who compares the beauty of Helen to that of a Cypress. Following up this idea, a reason for keeping evergreen and other

6

A FARM-YARD FOWL AT COMPTON WYNYATES

A "LEATHERN BOTTEL" CUT IN BOX AT COMPTON WYNYATES

trees closely clipped is apparent. From the mere clipping of these subjects so as to keep them in harmony with the architecture, to the cutting of evergreens into fantastic shapes, is not a very wide transition, but whether the latter style was first adopted by the Grecian or the Roman gardeners does not appear.

We do know, however, that the Romans practised Topiary freely and that they were also fine architects and builders. Even in the formation of sheltering groves of forest trees to provide welcome shade from the bright sunshine, the Romans adopted the formal quincunx method of disposing the trees. How much more, then, would they have been ready in that age of undeveloped taste in the design and planting of gardens to welcome a method of training and culture that enabled them not only to bring the garden up to the mansion without any resultant loss of architectural effect, but also permitted them to carry architecture into the garden and apply it in a more or less fantastic manner to the trees themselves.

On the authority of Martial we learn that the art of Topiary was first introduced to the Romans by Cneus Matius. Matius was the friend of Julius Cæsar and a particular favourite of Augustus, but whether he originated or borrowed the idea we know not. As a court favourite, however, he must have had ample opportunity for propagating this particular method of gardening, and doubtless then, as now, a fashion set at court was quickly followed by all who wished to be up-to-date. Good or bad, the taste spread, and even such a man of taste and letters as Pliny the Roman Consul considered it quite the proper thing to use Topiary work extensively in his famous Tuscan Villa. In a letter written by Pliny the Younger to his friend Apollinaris (Ep. v. 6) is a fine description of this garden. Melmoth's translation pictures the front

of the Portico as opening on to a sort of Terrace
" embellished with various figures, and bounded with
a Box Hedge, from which you descend by an easy
slope, adorned with the representation of divers animals
in Box, answering alternately to each other: this is
surrounded by a walk enclosed with tonsile evergreens,
shaped into a variety of forms.   Behind it is the
Gestatio, laid out in the form of a Circus, ornamented
in the middle with Box, cut into numberless different
figures, together with a plantation of shrubs prevented
by the shears from running too high: the whole is fenced
in by a Wall, covered with Box, rising in different
ranges to the top."   After dealing with trees, roses,
etc., he continues: " Having passed through these
winding alleys, you enter a straight walk, which breaks
out into a variety of others divided off by Box hedges.
In one place you have a little meadow ; in another the
Box is cut into a thousand different forms ; sometimes
into letters expressing the name of the master; sometimes that of the artificer ; whilst here and there little
Obelisks rise intermixed alternately with fruit trees,
when on a sudden you are surprised with an imitation
of the negligent beauties of rural Nature, in the centre
of which lies a spot surrounded with a knot of dwarf
Plane Trees."

It must not, however, be assumed that the Romans
were entirely without appreciation of natural beauty and
scenery. Far from it. But they loved lavish displays
of art, and this also led them to use the gardens immediately surrounding their dwellings as a gallery in
which to arrange their collections of sculptured trees.
Roman poets and philosophers alike have left in their
writings ample evidence that the beauties of nature
were greatly admired by their countrymen, but at that
period, when Rome was the mistress of the world,
Italy was well supplied with natural sylvan scenery, and

LEVENS GARDENS: THE BROAD WALK

consequently, where it was not at all necessary to cultivate this particular form of gardening, the desire for contrast and display led to a very widespread adoption of the art of Topiary.

From the gardens of the wealthy Romans the taste for clipped trees and general formality of design was carried throughout the Empire. Doubtless the monks who carried the arts of gardening throughout the European continent took with them and put into practice a taste for Topiary. In their wall-encircled monastic gardens dense hedges would rise both for the provision of shelter and to afford additional seclusion, and in a modest way these would in all probability be embellished by verdant sculptures.

But it was much later than this that Topiary commenced to be one of the chief features of garden design, for with the corruption of the ruling powers came the decline of the Roman Empire, and then followed the Dark Ages wherein the clash of arms, coupled with deep superstition, put gardening, as a pleasure, out of the question, so that except in some few cases it was only conducted at all because of the necessity of providing a meagre food supply. For long, long years war-like occupations were, either from choice or necessity, in the ascendant. But there presently came a time when peace again reigned and arts and commerce flourished; gardening revived, and in Italy where still remained many examples of the grandeur of Ancient Rome, it soon flourished in the establishments of the wealthy princes.

Although Charlemagne revived the art of gardening in France in the eighth century, he was not the kind of man to care much for garden display; he rather introduced useful fruits and encouraged the cultivation of herbs and fruits wholly from an economic point of view. So we are compelled by the lack of historical information to pass on to much later times ere we can again take up the tale of Topiary.

Loudon points out that the Roman style of gardening was lost in England when the Romans abandoned this country at the beginning of the fifth century, but he surmises that, following the revival of gardening in France by Charlemagne, William the Conqueror would probably re-introduce it at the end of the eleventh century. Some little progress was made in the reigns of Henry I. and Henry II., and it was the former who formed the Park at Woodstock (1123), probably the first of which there is any record. In accord with the prevailing taste, it contained a labyrinth, which appears to have chiefly constituted the Bower so intimately associated with the fate of Rosamund.

But during the twelfth century there was very little of either design or taste in the arrangement of gardens. These latter were of limited extent and, because of the feudal broils that enlivened the monotony of existence, they were for the most part attached only to the larger establishments, and in them were confined within the Glacis, or first line of defence, which was a necessity of the times. Beyond the inevitable moat, orchards arose, wherein the horticulturally inclined among the baron's retainers could indulge their taste for ornamental gardening; a taste which consisted then, according to Johnson, and continued to a much later age, "in having plants cut into monstrous figures, labyrinths, etc."

So common a part of garden design did labyrinths and mazes become at this period and during the thirteenth century, that we find scarcely a plan among the many given by De Cerceau in his "Architecture," issued about 1250, in which either a round or a square one does not appear. This brings us into the thirteenth century, an age wherein the taste for architecture and gardening spread northwards and especially took a firm hold in Holland,

BOATS, PYRAMIDS AND PEACOCK

where then, and later, the wealthy merchant princes liberally encouraged almost all branches of horticulture. Thus encouraged the florists entered heartily into the business of supplying their patrons, and, aided by a suitable climate and the various inventions born of necessity, they made Holland famous throughout the world for its commercial horticulture. So careful, however, were the Dutch of every inch of land, much of it reclaimed, that they laid out their gardens with mathematical precision and consequent primness, carrying this principle into the very trees and plants themselves.

It was in the early part of the fourteenth century that Pierre de Crescent, of Bologna, wrote his work on Agriculture, wherein he describes the kinds of pleasure gardens suitable for various classes of the community, and a suggestion of formality of design and the use of Topiary is made in his observation that a royal garden should contain a menagerie, and also an aviary placed among thickets, arbors and vines.

GOLDEN AGE OF TOPIARY

"I confess that I should never care to adorn my garden with topiary or with carpet bedding; but I hope always to be cautious in making declarations in respect of such matters, that I may not appear to despise another man's pleasures, or vainly desire to set up a standard of my own in opposition to the delightful variety that is ensured by the free exercise of individual taste and fancy."—*Shirley Hibberd.*

"While perhaps not admiring these birds and beasts, we must, I think, in a measure agree with Loudon, that many old-fashioned gardens have suffered in losing the quaint forms of cropped yews, which added a certain charm to them."—*John Lowe, M.D.,* in "Yew Trees of Great Britain and Ireland."

THE dawn of the sixteenth century saw the commencement of what may be called the Golden Age of Topiary. It was also the beginning of an age of romance, of stirring deeds, of great discoveries; an age when men of genius were numerous, when history was being rapidly made, and when the art of gardening began to flourish freely. Though the times were stirring ones and there was not always "peace within our borders," commerce grew and wealth increased, so that gardening became more and more popular and steadily grew more and more elaborate in design. To the existing style were added the extravagances of the French and the formalities of the Dutch schools, but these things did not all come to pass at once.

It is most probable that the Old and Formal English Gardens as we know or imagine them, were the development of at least two hundred years, and probably the type had not been reached until the reign of Charles II., notwithstanding such gardens are frequently alluded to

THE HARLINGTON YEW

(As clipped 1729 - 1790)

as Elizabethan. This idea seems the more reasonable after a perusal of Withington's " Elizabethan England," for though the Editor gives us Harrison's description of Gardens and Orchards, Woods and Marshes, Parks and Warrens, there is never a word that can be construed into a reference to Topiary, not even in his account of " the palaces belonging to the prince."

Nevertheless, quaint gardens were formed before the time of Elizabeth, Shakespeare, Drake, Raleigh, and Gerard. A curious conceit in these old-time gardens was the formation of a mound in the pleasure grounds, where none previously existed, and this seems to have been quite the correct thing in the way of garden design even as late as Evelyn's day, for we learn that he arranged for a " mountaine " in the family gardens at Wotton, in Surry. Leland, in his " Itinerary " (1540), refers to this feature in garden design in connection with the garden at Wrexhill Castle, near Howden, in York-shire. He says : " The Gardens within the mote, and the Orchardes without were exceeding fair. And yn the Orchardes were mounts, opere topiorii, writhen about with degrees like the turnings in cokil shelles, to come to the top without payn."

That Topiary had already a considerable hold upon the garden-loving public at this early date cannot be doubted. Very few of these ancient gardens remain unaltered at the present time, but in that most interesting book, " A history of Gardening in England," the Hon. Alicia Amherst gives the plans of Sir Henry Dryden's gardens at Canons Ashby, Northamptonshire, which show that clipped yews are prominent features, as two rows of four trees each line one of the approaches, and these trees have a diameter of about ten feet. The author states that this garden, originally made in 1550, was altered in 1708, " and has defied the changes of fashion for nearly two centuries."

Gerard (1545-1607), the famous old Herbalist who was gardener to Lord Burghley in the reign of Elizabeth, does not enlighten us as to the use of clipped trees, but Parkinson, another and equally famous Herbalist, who was born in 1567 and died about 1640, does give us a little information on the subject. Parkinson was Apothecary to James I., and Charles II. made him Botanicus Regius Primarius; he therefore had the advantage of exceptional opportunities for studying the plants of his time and their uses. Indeed some of the quaintest things ever printed are the accounts of the " Virtues" of the several parts of the plants described by Parkinson and by Gerard. Pointing out that the yew was largely used both for " shadow and an ornament," Parkinson seems to regret that the privet had not received proper attention at the hands of Topiarists simply because of its widespread use as a hedge plant, and he advocates its further employment by remarking that " to make hedges or arbours in gardens . . . it is so apt that no other can be like unto it, to be cut, lead, and drawn into what forme one will, either of beasts, birds, or men armed or otherwise."

Because of its comparatively slow rate of growth the yew has been the subject usually employed by topiarists, while box is a good second in point of popularity. Both these trees or shrubs have the additional merit of longevity. Wordsworth points out both the slow growth and longevity of the yew in his lines :—

> " There is a yew-tree, pride of Lorton Vale,
>   Which to this day stands single, in the midst
>   Of its own darkness, as it stood of yore,
>   Not loth to furnish weapons for the bands
>   Of Umfraville or Percy ere they marched
>   To Scotland's heaths ; or those that crossed the sea
>   And drew their sounding bows at Azincour,
>   Perhaps at earlier Crecy, or Poictiers.
>   Of vast circumference and gloom profound
>   This solitary tree !—a living thing

PEACOCKS, TABLES, SPIRALS AND BOATS IN YEW AND BOX AT J. CHEAL AND SONS, CRAWLEY

Produced too slowly ever to decay ;
Of form and aspect too magnificent
To be destroyed."

Heslington, near York, still boasts an ancient Topiary garden, where all the clipped trees are of yew. This, as well as the clipped hedges of Rockingham, and the hedges and clipped trees at Erbistock, date, according to the Hon. Alicia Amherst, from about 1560. Other trees and shrubs were also used by the tonsile artists, and even Rosemary was not omitted. Barnaby Googe (about 1578) observed that the women folk planted it and trimmed it into shapes " as in the fashion of a cart, a peacock, or such things as they fancy."

William Harrison, Rector of Radwinter, and Canon of Windsor, who wrote " A Description of England " contained in " Holinshed's Chronicles," has already been referred to. He was a most observant man and one who in his own picturesque language " had an especiall eye unto the truth of things " ; from 1586 to 1593 he was Canon of Windsor, and therefore anything he has to say about gardens is of unusual interest. His keen patriotism shines brightly through all his writings, and his high opinion of his own land is not in any way reduced when he comes to discourse upon gardens, for he writes : " I am persuaded that, albeit the gardens of the Hesperides were in times past so greatly accounted of, because of their delicacy, yet, if it were possible to have such an equal judge as by certain knowledge of both were able to pronounce upon them, I doubt not but he would give the prize unto the gardens of our days, and generally over all Europe, in comparison of those times wherein the old exceeded."

Early in the succeeding century, however, we come upon some more positive evidence of the use of Topiary work. Lawson, in 1618, shows more clearly that Topiary had become an important branch of the art of gardening, and that the designs carried out by some of the artists were, to say the least of it, remarkable. As indicative of the progress already made, he states: " Your gardener can frame your lesser wood to the shape of men armed in the field, ready to give battell : or swift-running Grey Hounds to chase the Deere, or hunt the Hare. This kind of hunting shall not waste your corne, nor much your coyne."

In the reign of Charles II. (1669-1685), garden design and garden ornamentation reached a degree of extravagance not previously attempted and not subsequently repeated. This was the time when Le Notre rose to be the most famous gardener in Europe, a time when Louis XI. was King of France (1643-1715). During this period there was a great striving after effect on the part of all possessed of ample means, while both aristocrat and plebeian desired and loved to be dazzled by brilliance or enchanted by the novel and singular. From Johnson we learn that during a residence at the court of France, Charles II. became enamoured of the French style of ornamental gardening introduced by Le Notre. This style differed chiefly from that already in vogue in its magnificence ; everything was carried out more elaborately and regardless of expense. " The alleys were lengthened, but still there were alleys, jets d'eau, mazes, parterres and statues, clipt trees and mathematically formed borders as of yore." It is said that the extravagance in garden ornamentation at Versailles was designed and carried into effect by Le Notre at a cost of two hundred million francs, or over £8,250,000. The great features were huge marble-edged water-basins, elaborate fountains, an abundance of masonry for the terraces, and clipped yew and box, making a sum total described at a much later date by Mr Wm. Robinson, in his " Parks and Gardens of Paris " as " the deadly formalism of Versailles."

BEECH HEDGE AND BOWLING GREEN AT LEVENS

Charles II. encouraged elaborate garden design, and, with it, Topiary ; it was under his orders that Le Notre himself laid out the semi-circular garden at Hampton Court. Gibson, who made a tour of London gardens in the reign of the " Merry Monarch," shows by his writings that the chief features of these establishments were the terrace walks, evergreen hedges, " shorn shrubs in boxes," and orange and myrtle trees.

In the earlier part of the seventeenth century the gardens of Bilton and Chilham were designed, with an accompaniment of clipped trees, while later in the century Sir William Temple, who negotiated the triple alliance between England, Sweden, and the Netherlands, laid out a Dutch garden at Moor Park. He had a large affection for the Dutch style of gardening, but was nevertheless quick to see that big formal gardens and their elaborate designs and masonry cost more to maintain in prim order than many who possessed them could well afford. It was also about this time that the now famous Topiary garden at Levens Hall, in West-moreland, was laid out by Beaumont, one of Le Notre's disciples. According to the inscription under his portrait at Levens Hall, Beaumont was " Gardener to James II. and Colonel James Grahme. He laid out the gardens at Hampton Court and at Levens." It was probably in some alteration of the Hampton Court gardens that Beaumont took part.

Topiary gardening reached its height during the reign of William and Mary (1689-1702). William III., Prince of Orange, brought with him a taste for clipped yews, and also for elaborately designed iron gates and railings. He accentuated the prevailing taste. Turning again to Johnson, we find garden design " was now rendered still more opposed to nature by the heavy additions of crowded hedges of Box, Yew, etc., which, however, by rendering the style still more ridiculous, perhaps hastened the introduction of a more natural taste which burst forth later." Some further idea of the prevalence of clipped trees is obtained from Celia Fiennes, who, in her chronicles of a journey " Through England on a Side Saddle in the time of William and Mary," makes frequent reference to alleys of clipped trees and to yew and cypress cut into " severall forms." William III. commenced the Kensington Gardens, and to alter a disfiguring gravel pit he employed the services of those famous Brompton nurserymen, London and Wise. In our time such a spot would in all probability be converted into a dell, with water and rock gardens, but London and Wise erected a mimic fortification, making the bastions and counterscarps of clipped yew and variegated holly. That this production was " long an object of wonder " can be easily understood, though whether it was one for " admiration " is open to question, notwithstanding that it had many admirers and was known as the " Siege of Troy."

Vegetable sculpture seems now to have reached its limit of popularity and design. Hazlitt, in his " Gleanings in old Garden Literature," hits off the situation admirably when he writes : " But it was to the Hollanders that London and his partner were indebted for that preposterous plan of deforming Nature by making her statuesque, and reducing her irregular and luxuriant lines to a dead and prosaic level through the medium of the shears. Gods, animals, and other objects were no longer carved out of stone ; but the trees, shrubs and hedges were made to do double service as a body of verdure and a sculpture gallery."

Evelyn, the celebrated diarist, who lived throughout the greater part of the seventeenth century, and just over five years of the eighteenth, strongly censured the prevalent method of clipping fruit trees into regular form, as well he might, but he claimed to be the first

EARLY EIGHTEENTH CENTURY VIEW OF LORD HAMILTON'S GROUNDS NEAR THE THAMES

to bring the yew into fashion for hedges, declaring it to be " as well for a defence as for a succedaneum to cypress, whether in hedges or pyramids, conic spires, bowls or what other shapes." And further he adds, " I do again name the yew, for hedges, preferably for beauty and a stiff defence, to any plant I have ever seen." Evelyn's residence from 1652 to 1694 was Sayes Court, Deptford, a home made famous to students of history because of its occupation by Peter the Great, of Russia, in 1698, to whom it was sub-let by Admiral Benbow. Peter the Great did not take the same care of the garden as Evelyn had taken, and his destruction, in part at least, of a famous holly hedge, caused the owner to regard the Russian Czar as a " right nasty tenant." An old writer informs us, with reference to Sayes Court, that Evelyn had " a pleasant villa at Deptford, a fine garden for walks and hedges, and a pretty little greenhouse with an indifferent stock in it. He has four large round philareas, smooth clipped, raised on a single stalk from the ground, a fashion now much used. Part of his garden is very woody and shady for walking ; but not being walled, he has little of the best fruits."

The beginning of the end was not now far to seek. One of our greatest modern landscape gardeners, Mr H. E. Milner, has written : " Precise designs of clipped box and yew are not out of place, if the building has a character that is consonant with such an accompaniment." Not satisfied with a few clipped trees in suitable positions, or with a part of the garden devoted to examples of Topiary, owners and gardeners alike, in the times I have briefly reviewed, seemed to have laboured to fill their gardens with illustrations of geometric figures, in box or yew ; with the quaintest patterns and wierdest shapes, caricaturing birds and beasts, and imitating architecture and things of common use. Distorted vegetation met the eye everywhere, and there was little of the natural and beautiful to relieve the general monotony. It was the excessive use of Topiary that led to its own downfall and caused Batty Langley to ask, " Is there anything more shocking than a stiff, regular garden ? "

CRUSADE AGAINST TOPIARY

"The Dutch Garden in front of Hampton Court Palace is unobjectionable, because it is in character with that part of the building and as a royal garden it ought to remain as it is, were it only to serve as an illustration of the style of gardening in the time of William and Mary."—*Charles M'Intosh.*

WHENEVER a fashion runs to extremes its end is not far to seek. On the one hand, a fashion becomes too general for those who have a taste for novelty, and especially for those who can afford at almost any cost to have something not available to the general public.

On the other hand, a fashion carried to excess becomes inconvenient and ridiculous, therefore it at once becomes offensive to those who are regarded as having good taste. And so it came about that when Topiary work had spread itself over all the gardens of the time and could hardly go further either in extent or design, there came the inevitable reaction. The same sort of thing has happened even in quite modern times.

One need not be very old to have seen the famous trained specimen plants that used to grace the highly successful exhibitions at the Royal Botanic Society's gardens, at the Crystal Palace, and elsewhere. Yet these giants have passed away, and in their places we have larger stocks of smaller and more easily grown subjects—in other words, the fashion has changed. "Bedding-out" reached such a height of fashionable popularity that it threatened to exclude the beautiful hardy perennial flowers from many a garden; it taxed the patience and ingenuity of the gardener and the purse of the employer almost to breaking point—it passed from reasonableness to absurdity. Then came a new order of things; perennials have been brought back and improved; hardy flowers are the fashion.

When Topiary threatened to exclude all else from the garden there arose several apostles of freedom, and these conducted a crusade against the art. Among those whose writings are more or less regarded in these days mention may be made of three—Bacon, Addison, and Pope.

The former early raised a protest, for in the times of Shakespeare and Queen Elizabeth, when Topiary was the prevailing taste if not the general fashion, he wrote, "I for my part do not like images cut in juniper or other garden stuff; they be for children." It was Bacon also who said: "As for the making of knots or figures that they may lie under the windows of the house on that side which the garden stands, they be but toys; you may see as good sights many times in tarts." But, alas, Bacon was curiously inconsistent. He would away with Topiary, but he puts forward as the best type of a garden one that is square, enclosed in an arched hedge, "with a turret over every arch, and a cage of birds in each turret, and over every space between the arches some other little figure with broad plates of round coloured glass, gilt, for the sun to play on." Those who so aptly quote Bacon when they pour out the vials of their wrath upon Topiary through the medium of the public press, may also be further reminded that Bacon would have in his ideal garden a fountain "embellished with coloured glass and such things of lustre."

But however much we may chuckle over the inconsistencies of Bacon it must be remembered that the age in which he lived (1561-1626) was remarkable rather for ostentatious display than for good taste,—

MUNTHAM COURT, SUSSEX

as we count good taste,—and consequently his horticultural purview was limited and obscured.   As the
poet Mason puts it :—

> " The age of tourney triumphs, and quaint masques,
>   Glar'd with fantastic pageantry, which dimm'd
>   The sober eye of truth, and dazzled ev'n
>   The sage himself; witness the high arch'd hedge,
>   In pillar'd state by carpentry upborne,
>   With coloured mirrors deck'd, and prison'd birds."

Bacon was in many things far in advance of the
Tudor times in which he lived, so far indeed, in respect
of our present subject, that no outstanding protest
against Topiary appears to have been made by those
who endeavoured to promote sound public taste, until
nearly another century had elapsed.   Then the literary
genius of Addison was directed against the evils and
extravagances of his age.

ADDISON AND POPE

" Addison,
Thou polished sage, or shall I call thee bard,
I see thee come : around thy temples play
The lambent flames of humour, bright'ning mild
Thy judgment into smiles ; gracious thou com'st
With Satire at thy side, who checks her frown,
But not her secret sting."—*Mason*.

" With bolder rage
Pope next advances ; his indignant arm
Waves the poetic brand o'er Timon's shades,
And lights them to destruction ; the fierce blaze
Sweeps through each kindred vista, groves to groves
Nod their fraternal farewell and expire."—*Mason*.

ALTHOUGH Addison and Pope were contemporaries it
was the former who led the crusade against formal
gardening in general and the art of Topiary in particular. Less satirical than his one-time friend, Addison
nevertheless pointed out with remarkable clearness that
the gardens of the early part of the eighteenth century
were not nearly so beautiful as they might have been,
owing to the excessive use of clipped trees and the
extreme care which the gardeners of that time took to
secure the utmost regularity in their planting and
uniformity in design.

Addison was counted one of the most brilliant of the
Essayists of his time, and among the numerous con-
tributions made by him to the *Spectator* is a lengthy one
" On the Pleasures of the Imagination." This took the
form of eleven Papers, or epistles, published in regular
order from June 21, to July 3, 1712. It is in the
fourth paper that he deals more particularly with

24

YEW TREE WITH BIRD

gardens and therein he shows that the works of nature are more pleasant to the imagination than are those of art, and that the works of art are most pleasing the more closely they resemble those of nature. He does not openly denounce Topiary and other formal gardening, but with subtle skill contrasts it with a picture of a more natural style, and does so in a manner that enforces the beauty of the latter and indicates the origin of that taste in landscape gardening which many a gardener of the nineteenth century thought was peculiarly his own.

"We have observed," says Addison, "that there is generally in nature something more grand and august than what we meet with in the curiosities of art. When, therefore, we see this imitated in any measure, it gives us a nobler and more exalted kind of pleaure than what we receive from the nicer and more accurate productions of art. On this account our English gardens are not so entertaining to the fancy as those in France and Italy, where we see a large extent of ground covered over with an agreeable mixture of garden and forest, which represent everywhere an artificial rudeness, much more charming than that neatness and elegancy which we meet with in those of our own country. It might indeed be of ill consequence to the public, as well as unprofitable to private persons, to alienate so much ground from pasturage and the plough, in many parts of a country that is so well peopled, and cultivated to a far greater advantage. But why may not a whole estate be thrown into a kind of garden by frequent plantations, that may turn as much to the profit as the pleasure of the owner? A marsh overgrown with willows, or a mountain shaded with oaks, are not only more beautiful, but more beneficial, than when they lie bare and unadorned. Fields of corn make a pleasant prospect; and if the walks were a little taken care of that lie between them, if the natural embroidery of the meadows were helped and improved by some small additions of art and the several rows of edges set off by trees and flowers that the soil was capable of receiving, a man might make a pretty landscape of his own possessions."

Continuing, the Essayist adds : "Writers who have given us an account of China tell us the inhabitants of that country laugh at the plantations of our Europeans, which are laid out by the rule and line ; because they say, anyone may place trees in equal rows and uniform figures. They choose rather to show a genius in works of this nature, and therefore always conceal the art by which they direct themselves. They have a word, it seems, in their language, by which they express the particular beauty of a plantation that thus strikes the imagination at first sight, without discovering what it is that has so agreeable an effect. Our British gardeners, on the contrary, instead of humouring nature, love to deviate from it as much as possible. Our trees rise in cones, globes, and pyramids. We see the marks of the scissors upon every plant and bush. I do not know whether I am singular in my opinion, but for my own part, I would rather look upon a tree in all its luxuriancy and diffusion of boughs and branches, than when it is thus cut and trimmed into a mathematical figure ; and cannot but fancy that an orchard in flower looks infinitely more delightful than all the little labyrinths of the most finished parterre. But, as our great modellers of gardens have their magazines of plants to dispose of, it is very natural for them to tear up all the beautiful plantations of fruit-trees, and contrive a plan that may most turn to their own profit, in taking off their evergreens, and the like movable plants, with which their shops are plentifully stocked."

It will be perfectly obvious that when Addison found it necessary to draw comparisons between a free and natural style of gardening, and the artificial methods carried out with mathematical precision in his time, to the distinct advantage of the former system, that geometric gardening, coupled with the excessive use of Topiary work, had made English gardens dreadfully monotonous. Essays were fashionable in the early years of the eighteenth century, and, remembering that their publication was extended over a considerable period, it must be presumed that they were freely read and discussed, and thus exerted a very considerable influence upon public opinion, just as a well thought out and carefully written leading article does in our own time. We may take it, then, that the gardeners of his time were considerably impressed by Addison's quiet denunciation of the existing style, and no doubt a revolution had already commenced in the minds, if not in the gardens, of the wealthy, when, a little more than a year later, Pope published in the *Guardian* (Tuesday, September 29, 1713), his famous essay on " Verdant Sculpture."

Not so subtle in his irony nor so engaging in his literary style as Addison, Pope was however the more forcibly satirical, maliciously spiteful, and elfishly humorous. His keen wit seized upon the proper psychological moment for following up Addison's comparatively mild exposure with an attack that did as much as, or more than, anything else to bring about that rapid decline of Topiarian art that quickly followed. Pope had evidently the genius of a great soldier, who delivers his fiercest attack when the enemy is wavering.

As Pope's essay is not by any means well known, neither is it especially easy of access, I need not apologise for quoting freely from it. Pope, however, believed with Dryden that satire was—

> " The boldest way, if not the best,
> To tell men freely of their foulest faults,'
> To laugh at their vain deeds and vainer thoughts,"

and in the course of his essay he allowed his sarcastic mockery to find expression here and there in a manner common enough in his time but which would be likely to offend the ears of modern polite folk, consequently I have in a few instances forestalled the editorial blue-pencil.

"I lately," writes Pope, "took a particular friend of mine to my house in the country, not without some apprehension that it could afford little entertainment to a man of his polite taste, particularly in architecture and gardening, who had so long been conversant with all that is beautiful and great in either. But it was a pleasant surprise to me, to hear him often declare, he had found in my little retirement that beauty which he always thought wanting in most of the celebrated seats, or, if you will, villas, of the nation. This he described to me in those verses, with which Martial begins one of his epigrams :

> "'Our friend Faustinus' country seat I've seen :
> No myrtles, placed in rows, and idly green,
> No widow'd plantain, nor clipp'd box-tree, there
> The useless soil unprofitably share ;
> But simple nature's hand, with nobler grace,
> Diffuses artless beauties o'er the place.'

"There is certainly something in the amiable simplicity of unadorned nature, that spreads over the mind a more noble sort of tranquillity, and a loftier sensation of pleasure, than can be raised from the nicer scenes of art."

After a reference to Homer's account of the Garden of Alcinous, and Sir William Temple's remarks upon it, Pope proceeds: "How contrary to this simplicity is the modern practice of gardening! We seem to make it our study to recede from Nature, not only in the various tonsure of greens into the most regular and formal shapes, but even in monstrous attempts beyond

CROWN GARDEN, MUNTHAM COURT, SUSSEX

the reach of the art itself. We run into sculpture, and are yet better pleased to have our trees in the most awkward figures of men and animals, than in the most regular of their own.

> " ' Here interwoven branches form a wall,
> And from the living fence green turrets rise ;
> There ships of myrtle sail in seas of box ;
> A green encampment yonder meets the eye,
> And loaded citrons bearing shields and spears.'

" I believe it is no wrong observation, that persons of genius, and those who are most capable of Art, are always most fond of Nature : as such are chiefly sensible, that all art consists in the imitation and study of nature. On the contrary, people of the common level of understanding are principally delighted with the little niceties and fantastical operations of Art, and constantly think that finest which is the least natural. A citizen is no sooner proprietor of a couple of yews, but he entertains thoughts of erecting them into giants, like those of the Guildhall. I know an eminent cook, who beautified his country seat with a coronation dinner in greens ; where you see the champion flourishing on horseback at one end of the table, and the queen in perpetual youth at the other."

" For the benefit of all my loving countrymen of this curious taste, I shall here publish a catalogue of greens to be disposed of by an eminent town gardener, who has lately applied to me upon this head. He represents, that for the advancement of a polite sort of ornament in the villas and gardens adjacent to this great city, and in order to distinguish those places from the mere barbarous countries of gross Nature, the world stands much in need of a virtuoso gardener who has a turn to sculpture, and is thereby capable of improving upon the ancients of his profession in the imagery of evergreens. My correspondent is arrived to such perfection, that he cuts family-pieces of men, women, or children. Any ladies that please may have their own effigies in myrtle, or their husband's in horn-beam. He is a puritan wag, and never fails when he shows his garden, to repeat that passage in the Psalms, "Thy wife shall be as a fruitful vine, and thy children as olive-branches round thy table." I shall proceed to his catalogue, as he sent it for my recommendation.

"Adam and Eve in yew; Adam a little shattered by the fall of the tree of knowledge in the great storm: Eve and the serpent very flourishing."

"The tower of Babel, not yet finished."

"St George in box; his arm scarce long enough, but will be in condition to stick the dragon by next April."

"A green dragon of the same, with a tail of ground-ivy for the present. *N.B.* These two not to be sold separately."

"Edward the Black Prince in cypress."

"A laurestine bear in blossom, with a juniper hunter in berries."

"A pair of giants, stunted, to be sold cheap."

"A Queen Elizabeth in phylyrea, a little inclining to the green sickness, but of full growth."

"A topping Ben Jonson in laurel."

"Divers eminent modern poets in bays, somewhat blighted, to be disposed of, a pennyworth."

"A quickset hog, shot up into a porcupine, by its being forgot a week in rainy weather."

"A lavender pig, with sage growing in his belly."

"Noah's ark in holly, standing on the mount; the ribs a little damaged for want of water."

Such was the crusade against Topiary; in its train came swift destruction. Bridgeman and Kent were the landscape gardeners who, influenced by the writings of their time and desirous of instituting a new order

QUEEN ELIZABETH'S CROWN AND JUG, ELVASTON CASTLE

of things, brought about the great change in garden design. They not only cleared away the sculptured trees but destroyed splendid, close hedges as well, throwing open to all eyes, and to all the winds, gardens that had hitherto been delightfully enclosed and secluded. Of Bridgeman there is very little information forthcoming, but Loudon tells us " He banished verdant sculpture and introduced morsels of a forest appearance in the gardens at Richmond." Kent was a versatile Yorkshireman, who was successively painter, architect and landscape gardener; Claremont, Esher, laid out about 1725-1735, was one of his designs. He was the friend of Lord Burlington and, even more than Bridgeman, he carried into effect the ideas of Pope. The great successor to Kent was Brown, who was head gardener at Stowe till 1750, and subsequently, after being employed by the Duke of Grafton, he was head gardener at Hampton Court and Windsor. At this time he became very much in request as a landscape gardener, and so continued well on towards the end of the eighteenth century. His sympathy with Topiary may be gathered from the remark made by Sir Wm. Chambers in 1772, that " unless the mania were not checked, in a few years longer there would not be found three trees in a line from Land's End to the Tweed." In the course of about fifty years, from 1740 to 1790, the gardens of England, with a few exceptions, were completely altered, and the style that had been in vogue for full one hundred and fifty years was almost wholly obliterated. Later designers added many improvements, and a more graceful style succeeded that of Kent and Brown, but Topiary as a part of garden design was practically non-existent for about a hundred years. Then commenced the modern revival of the Art.

REVIVAL OF THE ART

"There is a tendency to restore some of the screens which formed so characteristic a feature of the Dutch style, with a view to obtain a greater degree of privacy, and more shelter for both visitors and plants. With this restoration of sheltering hedges and verdant belts has evidently come a desire for examples of Topiary art, and already there are several modern gardens where they are to be found firmly established."—*George Gordon, V.M.H.*

"Topiary Work fell into disrepute in the nineteenth century, owing to the persistence with which the more natural styles of gardening came to the front, but even now this phase of ' gardening ' exercises a considerable fascination upon a large section of the public; witness the interest excited of late years by the exhibits of trimmed trees which have appeared at the London shows."—*Walter P. Wright.*

NOTWITHSTANDING the wonderful alteration and improvement that have taken place in British gardens since Kent began to make a clearance of Topiary work, several notable collections survived the general slaughter and these are to-day among the most interesting of the varied forms of gardening seen in the country. The gardens at Levens Hall and at Elvaston Castle may be especially particularised in this connection, but for the moment we will deal with the revival rather than the survival of the art.

During the past twenty years the practice of including at least a few specimens of clipped trees in any new garden of pretensions has been steadily growing, and within the last ten years several Topiary gardens of considerable extent have been laid out and planted. These are chiefly in the large establishments of the wealthy patrons of horticulture, and they are so situated

HENS, DUCKS, PEACOCKS, ETC., IN BOX AND YEW AT J. CHEAL AND SONS, CRAWLEY

that they are in harmony with formal surroundings, or disposed where they form a distinct item of horticultural interest and do not in any way mar the more natural beauties of adjacent subjects.

Precisely why there has been a revival of this old art I am not prepared to say. It must suffice that there is such a revival, and a very distinct one, as any one who visits gardens and exhibitions and nurseries frequently will readily discover. At the leading London and provincial exhibitions two old established firms of nurserymen have frequently and extensively exhibited examples of Topiary; these are Messrs Wm. Cutbush & Son, Highgate, N., and Messrs J. Cheal & Sons, Crawley, Sussex; and it may be safely asserted that if there were no taste or demand for clipped trees the respective proprietors would not incur the necessarily heavy expense of displaying this particular line of goods.

In the revival of Topiary in England no single person has taken a deeper interest than Mr Herbert J. Cutbush, and though his interest is confessedly a business one it is none the less worthy of mention. For many years Mr H. J. Cutbush has frequently visited Holland and he has travelled through and through the little country until he knows it, horticulturally, far better than even many eminent Dutch nurserymen do. He discovered that some of the best trained and best furnished specimens of sculptured yew and box were to be found in the farmhouse gardens, in small, almost unknown villages, far from the usual routes of tourists and business-men, and this led to still further explorations. During the first years of the revival Mr H. J. Cutbush crossed over to Holland nearly every week end making himself acquainted with the farmers, and with the few growers who regularly supplied the Dutch nursery trade. He got to know where examples were being steadily developed, securing options on these and purchasing all that were well advanced. As already hinted, the Dutch "Boomkmeckers," or nurserymen who cultivate clipped trees as a special business, are by no means a numerous class, they chiefly reside in the Boskoop district.

Churches of box and peacocks of yew are not imported without the expenditure of a good deal of time and money, and obviously there is some risk in removing large examples. One big tree that for sixty years had been the chief ornament of a Dutch black-smith's garden was only purchased after a whole day spent in persuasion and the consumption of much Schiedam, and after the purchase was made another week was spent in lifting and packing and removing the tree to the London steamer.

There is a great variety of form in the Dutch clipped trees, but spires surmounted with birds seem to be among the most common and are as easy to produce as most. For these, and for the peacocks and the spiral or serpentine columns, yew is almost invariably used. Tables, with tops either circular, oval or square, may be had in box or yew, and the leg of the table may be plain or ornamented according to taste. The arm-chairs in box have quite a comfortable and inviting appearance. Sitting hens, geese, and ducks are common designs, and to protect the verdant poultry one may obtain equally verdant dogs, with or without kennels, but though the mastiff may be of quite ferocious mien he can be warranted not to bite ; more-over he will require very little in the way of food and the noise he makes will disturb no one.

Churches are quite common designs among topiarists, but it is interesting to notice that seldom is there a doorway provided, and obviously if there is no congrega-tion there will be no collection taken. The churchyard

VEW TREE WITH BIRD—ANOTHER FORM

is also provided for, inasmuch as verdant tombstones
and Latin crosses are grown in considerable numbers,
and some of these would be vast improvements upon
many of the ugly head-stones and other memorials of
a more solid character that crowd our graveyards.
Pyramids, mop-heads, and blunt cones are among the
commonest designs; they do not call for the exercise
of much ingenuity, but when these pyramidal trees are
cut into several regular and well graded tiers their cost
increases considerably. Another form of tree that
naturally suggests itself to the Dutch grower, who all
his life is used to water and boats, is that of a sailing
ship, or barge; but these are not so easy to evolve from
either box or yew, and they call for a good deal of
training in addition to the cutting and clipping necessary
to keep them shapely. Thin wires and a few light
bamboo rods usually complete the training outfit
necessary, but taking the whole range of topiarian
design, training, in the sense of tying out, is not much
practised.

Compared with the designs enumerated in the
catalogue that Pope's fancy created, the modern list
of verdant sculptures is a very modest one. True we
may have Jugs and Beakers, Wreaths as well as Crosses,
and Swans as well as Peacocks, varying in price from
three guineas to ten guineas each, but the moderns do
not attempt to pourtray Adam and Eve, nor do they
caricature the poets and statesmen of the age, in living
box and yew.

Prices are governed chiefly by the size and age
(height and density), and the design of the specimen.
The yew tree being of slower growth than the box is,
size for size, the most expensive of the two, and well
furnished examples that have not exceeded marketable
size vary in age from twenty to sixty years. Even when
designed in box the birds are about ten or twelve years

old, dogs twelve to fourteen years, and taller designs
from fifteen to eighteen years. Some of the finer
examples found in the country districts of Holland need
to have their root system cut around one year, so that
they may be safely lifted, transported to this country
and transplanted in the following season.

It may very reasonably be asked, Where are to be
seen the signs of this modern revival of Topiary, apart
from horticultural exhibitions ? To that I make answer
by pointing to some establishments famous throughout
the land for their gardens. At Ascott, Mr Leopold de
Rothschild has a thoroughly well furnished and quite
modern Topiary Garden, and those who are disposed to
severely criticize the modern revival of an old garden
art must bear in mind that Mr Rothschild's gardens at
Gunnersbury and Ascott have been and are still being
referred to as fine examples of the most advanced and
tasteful style of natural and adapted gardening. Another example is to be found at Friar Park, Henley-on-
Thames, the residence of Mr Frank Crisp. This is a
comparatively new garden but it contains much that is
beautiful and a very great deal that is interesting, and
its collection of clipped trees is not the least interesting
feature of an establishment that also contains one of the
best collections of alpine plants in the Southern Counties.

If these are not sufficient answer to the question, I
hasten to add Witley Court, Stourport, the residence of
Lady Dudley ; and Danesfield, Marlow, the home of Mr
R. W. Hudson. Besides these there are numerous other
gardens throughout the land where Topiary, as a modern
development, occupies no mean position, the extent of
the collections of clipped trees being determined chiefly
by the space at disposal.

CLIPPED YEWS AT A COTTAGE ENTRANCE

THE FORMATION OF A TOPIARY GARDEN

THE Topiary, Dutch, or Formal Garden, as it is sometimes called, belongs to a period long since gone by. It is uncertain who was the first person to introduce the formal garden into England, and it is doubtful whether this style of gardening had its origin in Holland or in France.

The present Gardens of Levens Hall were laid out between the years 1701 and 1704; but it is pretty certain that the art of Topiary gardening was practised in England before the gardens at Levens were remodelled in that style.

Before the year 1704, Monsieur Beaumont, who had been already employed by King James II. to lay out the gardens of Hampton Court Palace, was engaged by Colonel James Graham, at that time Treasurer to James II., to introduce the art of Topiary work into his gardens at Levens, and it is probable that these two places were the first in this country in which the genuine art was practised. Beaumont, it may be mentioned, was a pupil of the famous Le Notre.

The laying out of any garden in which clipped trees are intended to be the principal feature, is open to a serious objection—the only objection, as I think, that can reasonably be entertained against Topiary work. I allude to the very great length of time it takes to bring the Topiary Garden to perfection. It is certain that the individual who takes both trouble and pains to lay out his garden can never expect to see his work perfected; for, even in its natural state, the yew is an extremely slow-growing tree, and when it is subjected to continual clipping and pruning year after year, its growth is considerably impeded.

But, even after allowing for this objection, I think it is a style of gardening that should be more encouraged, and, if possible, made more popular than it is at the present time. I am fully aware that there are many authorities in the gardening world who condemn the Formal Garden as unnatural; but I am certain that there is a charm and a beauty of its own in Topiary work not to be met with in the modern garden. No doubt it would be a pity were every person's tastes to be alike, and fortunately opinions differ in gardening as in other matters.

We will suppose, however, that, notwithstanding the objections I have named, some reader of mine has decided to make for himself a Dutch, or Topiary Garden—for both styles are practically the same.

The choosing of a situation, if a choice can be had, is of primary importance. A place should be selected where the trees to be planted can obtain the fullest possible amount of sunlight. At the same time, it should be completely sheltered from every wind that blows.

It must be remembered that although the yew is a tree which will grow and flourish in almost any out-of-the-way corner when left alone in its natural state, it is quite a different matter when each individual tree in the garden is intended to be as fine and as perfect a specimen of Topiary work as it is possible to make it; and, like everything else in a Topiary garden, a tree should be trained as well as possible, or else let alone altogether.

It is very easy to perceive the great difference between trees which have been planted partly or wholly in the shade and those that have always enjoyed a full measure

CROSSES AND JUGS IN YEW

of sunlight. There is a strong and vigorous growth about the latter which is not to be found in those planted in a shady spot. It may not always be practicable to plant each tree in a garden where it will receive the full benefit of the sun ; but it is an object which should ever be kept in mind, and carried out as far as possible.

The yew is a tree which repays good treatment, especially when year after year it is subject to clipping and never suffered to grow in its natural state.

The situation chosen for a Topiary Garden should be a hollow, or piece of ground slightly sunk below the general level of the surrounding land. If this should be impracticable, it would be advisable to make a terrace on at least one side of the ground marked out for the garden, preferably the north side, as a terrace on the north side cannot interfere with the full benefit of the sun, or obscure it from the trees in any way. There is no place whence Topiary work is seen to greater advantage than from a terrace, or, indeed, from any elevated spot from which one can look down on the garden. A terrace, in my opinion, has a double recommendation, inasmuch as besides adding beauty to the garden it also affords good shelter ; and shelter is a necessary consideration. In fact it is of almost as much importance to provide efficient shelter as it is to get the greatest possible amount of sunlight, which I have always considered to be absolutely indispensable to the welfare of the various species of trees planted in a Topiary garden. Nothing is more injurious to the yew tree than strong winds from whichever direction they may happen to blow, and more especially are they hurtful if the garden be situated near the sea. If such be the case, and the garden be not well sheltered, the salt spray every now and then blown up even several miles inland, has a very deleterious effect on the trees. I have seen old and splendid specimens of the yew disfigured for several years from this cause alone ; and the older the tree the more damaging is the effect.   Whatever the kind of shelter provided, it should be planted, or erected, in such a way as not to obscure the general view of the garden.

Espaliers, with fruit-trees trained on them, were formerly used to a great extent in Topiary gardens; but they are a kind of shelter little to be recommended, as, though certainly not unsightly, and having the advantage of being useful, they are somewhat out of place and scarcely in keeping with other features of the garden.

Hardy flowering shrubs may always be planted. They make a very good shelter, and are at the same time ornamental, while they have the additional advantage of being useful for cutting purposes.

But in close proximity to the garden, there is nothing which affords more effectual shelter or is more in harmony with its general character than hedges of yew or horn-beam of about ten to twelve feet in height. This, as a rule, is quite high enough to answer the purpose of shelter ; if allowed to grow higher, the strength and substance of a hedge is almost certain to be sacrificed.   This, of course, applies in a greater degree to yew than to horn-beam.

Large timber trees, such as oak, lime, beech or sycamore, cannot very well be planted within the garden, though they may easily be so in the grounds, or even outside them.   They should not be planted singly, but either in large clumps or thick enough to form a wood which, in course of time, may afford shelter to the whole garden.

The next thing requiring the attention of the Topiary gardener, and one which must be considered in a special degree, is the general formation of the garden.   This is a matter of vital importance, and, in common with all branches of garden architecture, needs great forethought and technical skill.   In commencing a Dutch or Topiary

VARIOUSLY SHAPED YEW TREES

A PEACOCK CUT IN YEW AT COMPTON WYNYATES

garden, everything should be laid out in a formal way; always, of course, taking care to avoid unnecessary stiffness in design.

In the carrying out of the Topiary work, Man is striving to a very great extent against Nature, and Nature is never an easy adversary to fight. Natural beauty, therefore, must not be considered too deeply in the formal laying out of a Topiary garden. I am far from wishing to imply that Nature should be entirely neglected; but in the general formation and practical management of a Topiary garden, a quaint and unique appearance is the thing that must be aimed at, and sometimes even a grotesque effect. Hence Nature must occasionally be relegated to a secondary position. Natural beauties, however, appeal to everybody, and if it can be found possible to combine the two, so much the better.

If it is intended to lay out a garden in which plenty of space can be allowed for planting, let us say, a hundred or more trees, a large piece of ground will be found to be necessary. It is always advisable to devote plenty of ground to the work, as it is a great mistake to plant the trees too close together. Although the trees when in a small state may not appear to be crowded, if sufficient space has not been allowed for their growth and development, the garden will afterwards present a cramped and heavy appearance which will greatly mar its general effect as times goes on.

The system of planting entirely in grass is not, I think, to be greatly recommended, although a few single trees planted here and there on the lawns may look well. For various reasons which shall be explained hereafter, I believe it to be better to combine the Topiary proper and the flower-garden.

When it has been decided how many trees it is intended to plant, and how much space is available for the work, the ground should be mapped out in six or eight large squares or quarters. These squares need not be all of one uniform size, or of exactly the same shape. As a general rule, the person who is laying out the garden will have to be guided by circumstances as regards the shape and size of these divisions.

There are so many different designs of garden architecture that it is of very little use trying to describe any particular form. I would recommend, however, that the design chosen be as simple a one as possible. The flower-beds should be made of rather a large size, and afterwards may be planted with roses, and herbaceous and bedding plants; they will also serve the additional purpose of containing the clipped trees. I do not, of course, mean that all the beds should be of uniform size or shape; but the beds in which trees are to be planted should be from twenty-five to forty feet in length, and from five to seven feet wide. A bed of these dimensions will be found to answer all purposes fairly well, whatever be the design adopted, and whatever shape may be given to the beds themselves.

All the paths, with the exception of the main walks between the quarters or divisions, should be grass; and those main walks should have a substratum of some hard material and be covered on the surface with loose gravel. Some objection may be raised to grass walks as being of an unserviceable nature for general garden work; but, if the main walks are made as suggested, the amount of work and trampling on the grass paths will be reduced to very small proportions, and even when necessary to do any heavy work over the latter, such as wheeling manure or other traffic of a similar nature, dry or frosty weather can usually be chosen as the most convenient moment.

In making the flower-beds, box should always be used for edging; never stones or ornamental tiles, as any-

OLD-FASHIONED BOX GARDEN, CHASTLETON HOUSE

thing of this description is altogether out of keeping with the general features of a Topiary garden. There may be a slight objection to box edging on account of the difficulty of getting it to grow well in certain soils. Generally speaking, I have never had the slightest difficulty in getting it to flourish and remain in a healthy condition, provided it gets proper treatment. I have some boxwood at Levens which has not been relaid for nearly, if not quite, a hundred years; and yet it is in a strong, healthy state.

When the portion of the garden intended to be devoted to Topiary gardening has been laid out, attention should be given to the other portion of the grounds; and, as none of the old formal gardens were considered to be complete without a bowling-green and hedges of yew, horn-beam, or holly, a bowling-green should be made and then enclosed by one or another of these species of hedge.

Any additional space not required for lawns or terraces should be made into fruit and vegetable quarters. If it can be found convenient to have the vegetable garden separate from the other, so much the better; as any space not absolutely required may then be utilised for fruit trees only. Old apple trees, with their gnarled stems and branches, with here and there a branch of mistletoe hanging among them, are picturesque objects enough among any surroundings.

In the grounds, as well as in the garden, grass walks should predominate between the hedges, and in the quarters devoted to fruit trees and vegetables. Indeed, wherever a path or walk is necessary, it should be grassed, if possible.

PLANTING AND MANURING

BEFORE planting operations are taken in hand, the beds should first be thoroughly prepared, and made ready for the reception of the trees. As with everything else connected with the management of a garden, a good beginning, followed by careful attention and proper treatment, generally means a successful result. Although the yew is a gross feeding tree, it will thrive fairly well in almost any poor soil ; but it is advisable only to plant in a soil of a nature that will, as far as possible, suit the requirements of the various trees it is intended to carry. Everything that can be done at this period to ensure the future success of the garden should be carefully attended to.

It must be borne in mind that a Topiary garden when completed will in all probability endure for an indefinite length of time—perhaps for hundreds of years. Any extra labour or expense devoted to the work of initiation will, therefore, be fully repaid in the future.

If the land that has been selected for the garden is composed of loam of a rich, mellow nature, all that is necessary will be to trench the ground two or three " spits " deep. If the soil is of a limestone composition it will be to the advantage of the yew trees, as these seem to grow well and vigorously in a soil of this kind. But if, on the other hand, the soil be of a poor, hungry nature, it will be advisable to remove it altogether, to the depth of two or three feet, replacing it with good loam of a more suitable character.

Nothing will answer this purpose better than the top

44

COTTAGE AT DITCHEAT, SOMERSET

" spit " off old pasture or meadow land. The top
" spit " only should be used, and this should not be
removed to a greater depth than five or six inches.
Turf taken off at this depth will generally contain all
that is best in the soil of either pasture or meadow land.

Although not absolutely necessary, it will be found
advantageous if the loam be obtained six or eight
months previous to the time when it will be required
for use. It should be removed from the fields, and
carefully stacked, in order to kill the grass and partially
decay the turf. Partially decayed loam is in all respects
better than that which has just been procured from the
fields. The trees make better roots in it, and it is
also easier to chop with the spade—a thing which will
be found necessary to do before it can be put on the
beds. The grass has also to be considered ; and unless
this is covered by a good depth of ordinary garden soil,
it will prove exceedingly troublesome during at least
the first year after planting. Of course, if the garden
be a large one, and operations can be carried out on
a large scale, the removal of the old soil and replace-
ment by other and more suitable loam will entail a
considerable amount both of labour and expense. But,
as I have before observed, nothing should be left
undone at this period of the work that will help to
ensure its future success.

There is, however, another and more simple method
of replacing the soil, and one which may answer the
purpose equally well. After the beds have been made,
the places may be marked out where it is intended to
plant the trees. The soil may then be removed and a
hole made of from four to five feet in diameter and from
two to three feet in depth, according to the size of the
tree it is proposed to plant. By following this method
the labour and cost of removing the entire soil from the
beds and replacing it with new loam will be to a great

extent reduced, and results obtained which should be almost, if not quite as satisfactory. The remaining soil left in the beds, no matter how poor it may be, can soon be made rich enough for either herbaceous or bedding plants by a liberal use of manure.

When the beds have been prepared for the reception of the trees, planting should be at once proceeded with, provided, of course, that the planting season be at hand. Like all other forms of tree-planting, it should be done as soon as possible after the proper time arrives ; or, to be more explicit, from the middle of October to the middle of November.

Although the work of lifting and transplanting yew trees and box can be carried on with perfect safety up to the end of the year or even up to the end of January, the earlier season is undoubtedly the better. The soil has then more chance to get settled about the roots before the advent of hard weather. I have seen yew trees lifted and transplanted even in June, but do not consider it to be by any means a suitable time for the work, and it is not a practice to be recommended. If left so late in the year as June, constant attention must be paid to watering, else the result will be disastrous.

If the trees have been growing for a few years in a reserve nursery-garden close at hand, they can be lifted and replanted without undue exposure to the open air or drying winds ; but if they have to be brought from afar, and have had to undergo a long railway journey, they are almost certain to be found on arrival to be dry at the roots. In this case, they should be at once un-packed and submerged in a tank of water for a few hours, and then heeled into the ground as near as possible to the place where planting is to be carried on, and after-wards lifted and replanted as required.

No rank manure of any kind should be used either mixed with the soil, or applied to the roots of the trees, or the result will be injurious. If manure of any kind be employed, nothing is better for the purpose than coarse bones used in moderate quantities—about one barrow load of bones to twenty or twenty-five barrows of loam.

It will be necessary to exercise great skill and fore-thought in arranging and planting the various trees with which it is intended to adorn the garden. Every-thing should be done to make the garden as unique, and at the same time as bright and attractive as possible. Now that such excellent varieties of golden yew are obtainable, a fairly large number of these should be planted. They should not, however, be allowed to predominate over the common green yew ; but if a few be planted, it will help to relieve the sombre appearance of the ordinary English yew.

Box is another kind of tree that lends itself admir-ably to Topiary work, and one that should not be forgotten during the planting period, as a few of the different varieties of box will greatly add to the general effect. There are also the different varieties of holly and golden privet ; but, as regards the former, unless it is purely for the sake of contrast, which is admired in all gardens, I should recommend its omission from the list of trees to be planted, as it does not lend itself to clipping. Its chief fault, however, is its untidy nature, which causes it to be a nuisance in a garden. It is perpetually shedding its leaves throughout the summer, when every garden should be looking its neatest.

No trees are more suitable for Topiary work than the different varieties of yew and the boxwood, as these are the most easily clipped and trained. Although the yew is an exceedingly slow-growing tree, it will, even with continual clipping, grow into a tree of large dimensions ; and, if the whole garden has been planted at one time, instead of adding trees at intervals of a few years, there will be too much uniformity about it. This should be avoided as far as possible, and if a few box trees have been planted here and there, they will help to break the evenness of the garden, since box can be kept down to almost any size desired by the aid of constant clipping.

When the work of marking out the places and planting the trees is being done, avoid anything that will afterwards have a tendency to over-crowding. Allow plenty of space for each tree to develop into whatever size or shape may be desired, and then have plenty of space for each tree to be plainly and distinctly seen. Trees that are too thickly planted never have the same appearance as those that have been allowed sufficient space; neither is over-crowding beneficial. It has a great tendency to draw the trees up too quickly, at the expense of strong and robust growth.

When the planting operations are finished, each tree should be given a good mulching of farmyard manure. Nothing is more beneficial to the health and vigour of the trees than half decayed manure from the farmyard, applied as a mulching either to old or newly-planted trees. It is the best stimulant that can be applied, as it answers the two-fold purpose of imparting health and vigour to the trees and protecting the roots from frost during winter, although there is perhaps very little danger of frost doing any damage to the roots of the yew on account of its extreme hardiness. It is always safer to protect trees that have been recently planted, and the manure will certainly not be wasted.

If the garden is an old established one and full of old trees, these will be greatly benefited by the aid of occasional top dressings of some sort of manure, or the trees will begin to show signs of deteriorating in course of time. More especially will top dressing be necessary

CROSS IN YEW OVER THE GRAVE OF LT.-GENERAL ARBUTHNOT, K.C.B., K.T.S., IN ST. BONIFACE CHURCHYARD, BONCHURCH, ISLE OF WIGHT

if the ground or beds where the trees are planted is not
liberally manured every year. But if manure is liberally
applied, the necessity for top dressing the roots will
not be so great; for the yew extends its roots for a
long distance and therefore absorbs a great deal of
whatever kind of manure is applied to the ground.
Although chemical manures may be used for the sake
of convenience, or lack of farmyard manure, they are
not strongly recommended. Of course if farmyard
manure cannot be obtained, then chemical manure of
some sort will have to be resorted to, but this will
not have the same desired effect in imparting vigour
to the trees. The principal objection to farmyard
manure arises on account of its unsightliness in the
garden; but that can be remedied to a great extent
by removing a few inches of soil from the roots and
applying a layer of the manure, and afterwards replacing
the soil. Liquid manure of any kind will be of the
greatest benefit to old trees, and there is no doubt that
chemical manure if applied to the roots at all, should
be given in liquid form during spring or summer, when
the weather is dry. It will greatly assist the trees in
making good growth.

The clipped yew is of such a close nature that it
takes very heavy rains to penetrate the roots.

MANAGEMENT OF OLD TREES

IT is perhaps when the work of clipping and training the trees begins, that the most difficult part of the practical management of a Topiary garden is experienced; but as in this chapter I intend to deal only with old trees, I will leave the training and shaping of young trees to be described in another chapter.

It is a matter that requires both skill and experience, both on the part of the man who is handling the shears, and of the gardener who is superintending, and who is also responsible for the work. There is nothing which looks worse in a garden than trees not properly clipped, and no clipped work can be called properly done if all or even any shear marks are visible to the eye. Clipping and training of trees in a Topiary garden is work that should either be done properly or else not at all. If the greatest possible amount of care is not bestowed on the trees, they will very soon grow out of shape, and, of course, become unsightly; and nothing is wanted in a garden that is not pleasing to the eye.

If the garden is a very extensive one and contains a large number of old specimen trees, the work of clipping them and cleaning up afterwards is an undertaking that requires a great deal of time and labour, as the work is not of a nature that will allow men to hurry over it, and it is moreover a labour of skill and patience.

In an old Formal Garden, where Topiary work is considered the principal feature, it is advisable to allow only men who are thoroughly experienced in the work to do the clipping. In fact, if the shape and symmetrical

YEWS AT MONTACUTE, SOMERSET

appearance of the trees are to be kept as nearly as possible perfect, experienced men are necessary. Of course, in any garden it will sometimes happen that the gardener may have to put a novice to do some part of the clipping, as fortunate indeed is the gardener in charge of a Topiary garden who can rely year after year on three or four men who are thoroughly trained and accustomed to the art of Topiary clipping. When it is found necessary to employ a person to do any part of the clipping who has not had any previous experience, he should only be allowed to begin on trees of the least importance, and those most concealed from view. The beginner will always find that a round or oval shaped tree is a great deal less difficult to work upon than a square one, or a hedge. Therefore, if possible, he should be allowed to get his hand in on round trees. It is always a wise plan when a novice is learning the work, to have a thoroughly experienced person working close at hand—but not on the same tree—to assist him and see that as few mistakes as possible are made. No hard and fast line can be drawn as to the exact date when the clipping season should begin, but it should be as soon as possible after the trees have completed their growth, as at that season the young shoots are soft, and not so difficult to clip. In any case it should not be later than the middle of September, especially if there is a large amount of clipping to be done. If it can be found convenient to start a fortnight or three weeks earlier, so much the better. More especially does this apply to beech or horn-beam, as they finish their growth sooner than the yew, and if they are not clipped immediately, the young shoots get hard and, of course, are more difficult to manage. Where there is enough clipping to keep three or four men at work for nine or ten weeks, the sooner the work is commenced after September comes in the better, as it enables the work to be got through

before the severe frosts of winter set in. When the
trees are of a large size—a thing that is generally the
case in old gardens—scaffolding of some sort will be
necessary, and for this purpose there is nothing better
than trestles made to close up into as little space as
possible, for the double purpose of storing them away in
winter or at any time they are not required for use, and
for the sake of convenience in carrying them about the
garden. The trestles should be made in at least three
different sizes, two of each size, or more if necessary.
These, with the aid of a single plank laid across two
equal sized trestles, will generally suffice for the work.
Of course, the plank that is used must be strong enough
to carry a man, and wide enough to give him plenty of
standing room.

If the trees are old and practically perfected in shape,
the work of clipping is not such a difficult matter as
when the trees are in course of training. But it is
usually the case that although many of the trees are old
there are young ones coming on that have to be shaped.
In the case of old trees, as a general rule, all that is
required is to take off the year's growth ; clipping back
to the old growth of the previous year.

Hard clipping of old trees is a practice that should to
a certain extent be carried out, unless it is desired to
enlarge the size of the tree. If this is the case, from
one inch and a half to two inches of the year's growth
should be left on, but not more.

Altering the shape of old trees is a thing that should
be avoided as far as possible, especially if the trees are
well shaped and in a healthy condition. It sometimes
happens that one or more trees in the garden may have
been allowed through careless management or some
other cause to grow out of shape ; or perhaps an old
tree may be obscuring the view in some way or other.
In the case of such a thing happening, it will be

THE POST OFFICE, DITCHEAT, SOMERSET

necessary to use the pruning knife or saw rather severely, both of which can be used with perfect safety when they are in the hands of a person who thoroughly understands the yew; provided, of course, he does not go to extremes, the yew is a tree that will stand a fair amount of rough treatment, and one that can be twisted and cut into almost any shape desired.

I have seen old specimen trees that had grown out of shape, or were, perhaps, shutting out the view in some part of the garden, taken down and re-trained, or cut down with the pruning saw, or knife, as the case might be; and yet in a very few years they had quite recovered and grown into nice, well shaped trees, full of vigour and well furnished with young growth. Rather will the tree, if it is carefully managed, be improved by the severe pruning it has been subjected to.

Of course, after an operation like the one I am describing, great care will have to be taken that every use is made of the young growth, as the main object to be kept in view is to get the tree well furnished again in as little time as possible. There will be very little, if any need for using the shears the first year after the cutting back has been done; but if the young growth is at all rank, it should be carefully thinned with an ordinary pruning knife, always taking care that only the weaker shoots are removed, leaving the stronger ones to grow for use another year, when they can be tied in and cover up, as far as possible, the old and bare wood. When tying young shoots, tarred string will be found most suitable. It answers the purpose very well and it is easier to tie than wire, although it has a tendency to decay quickly through being always exposed to the weather. In the case of young shoots the pressure is not great and string will generally last as long as the tie is required, as the shoots soon become matted and interwoven together;

but if a strong branch should happen to get displaced in any way, the use of string as a tying material should be avoided and copper wire should always be substituted in its place. In the case of an old branch the pressure is greater, and whatever material has been used in the work, it will as a rule be intended to last for years. For the purpose of tree tying of any description copper wire is to be recommended; it has not the same injurious effect on the trees as ordinary galvanised wire; but whatever is used, cork should always be placed between the wire and the wood as a preventive against cutting the tree.

When clipping an old tree that is a perfectly square one, it is a good practice to use either a line or some kind of straight edge. If the man who is doing the work uses one or the other he can generally give the tree a better and more finished appearance than if he trusts to the eye only.

Perhaps of all the different kind of shapes there are to clip in the Topiary garden, hedges require the most skill and care, and only the most experienced men should be allowed to undertake the work of clipping them. Hedges in the garden are mostly planted in such a way that their entire length is visible, and of course the most casual observer can see at a glance whether they are properly clipped or if there are any shear marks visible on them. If the hedge is composed mostly of curves, then of course the clipping is not such a difficult matter. A long, straight hedge and one that is almost entirely made up of curves, differ in the same respect with regard to the ease with which they can be clipped, exactly in the same way as a round or an oval tree. When clipping a straight hedge a person should never trust entirely to the eye, and lines should always be used; and for the purpose nothing is better than ordinary garden lines.

In the case of hedges that are cut into battlements

OLD EXAMPLE OF TOPIARY IN BOX AT COMPTON WYNYATES

at the top, these should have a line stretched length-ways along the ground, another along the base of the battlements, and another along the top of the battle-ments ; and whatever size and width the battlements are, say, for instance, two feet high and two feet in width between them, a stick cut exactly two feet in length or a two-foot rule should be used to measure the exact height and distance between the battlements ; and if those precautions are taken, any person with a fair knowledge of the art of clipping can hardly with ordinary care and attention get wrong ; as, after all, the work of clipping Topiary trees is not so difficult as might be expected.

There are several points that should always be remembered. Symmetry and shape are necessary to make a good tree ; and this may be said to be the first and most important factor in the work. Another point is to take particular care that the shears do not cut off more than is necessary. By that I mean, never to allow the shears to cut deep enough into the tree to make a hole. Another very important point to aim at is to give the tree as smooth and even an appearance as possible after the work is finished. I am perfectly aware that, in a large collection of yews or other clipped trees, there are always some that it is impossible to clip properly, on account of weak growth, or some other cause. For instance, trees that are growing in a part of the garden where they are fully exposed to wind and storm are almost certain to get into an unhealthy condition. The growth becomes weak and stunted, or perhaps the branches get worked out of place, or even die out altogether. In the case of trees of that description, no matter how much tying is done or how carefully they are clipped, they can never be made to have the same appearance as those that are full of young growth and are in a healthy and vigorous state.

Where the garden has been planted with mixed trees—such as yew, holly, boxwood and horn-beam, the clipping should all be done in the autumn so as to give the garden a tidy and uniform appearance. Autumn is not generally considered the right season of the year for holly clipping, but if there are some, more or less, planted among the yews in the Topiary garden, it is necessary that they should be clipped at the same time as the other subjects, for the sake of appearance. But if hollies are planted by themselves in some isolated part of the garden, whether in hedges or bushes, the work of clipping them should be carried out towards the latter end of May or beginning of June; then hard clipping every other year will suffice for them. At Levens we clip the holly hedges which are not actually in the Topiary garden hard back to the old wood every alternate year, and other years we merely go over them with a pair of shears and cut away the long shoots. I am rather of the opinion that hard clipping of hollies every year is more injurious than beneficial to the trees.

It is evident to anyone who has seen an old Dutch or Topiary garden, that, in the formation and laying out of the grounds, boxwood has always been considered one of the principal features, and in most of them it remains so to this day.

Where box succeeds well and remains in perfect health, no care or attention should be spared to keep it so, for there is no edging that can be used in the garden to be compared with it for beauty. It has, however, some drawbacks, the principal one of which is the excellent accommodation it affords to snails and other garden pests; but its advantages more than counter-balance its defects. Like the hollies, every other year is sufficient for clipping it, and there is no more suitable month for the work than June. There should be no clipping done to boxwood until all danger of frost is

LEVENS GARDENS: GENERAL VIEW

gone, as it is extremely dangerous to clip before that period has passed. There is nothing more injurious to newly clipped boxwood than sharp frosts. I have seen boxwood that was over a hundred years old clipped in April, with the result that a few sharp frosty nights killed the whole of it.

Excepting during the clipping season, there is very little work to be done to the trees in a Topiary garden, unless it is top-dressing them with some sort of manure, or keeping a look-out for branches that have become loose through wind or some other cause. If this occurs, the branches should be immediately tied back into their places before any injury takes place to the tree.

There is another danger that should be strictly guarded against in winter, and that is, the danger the trees undergo in the event of heavy falls of snow. When the trees are old and large and in every way adapted for carrying a heavy weight of snow, no time should be lost in getting it removed as quickly as possible; the sooner the men get to work the better, even before the snow has ceased if it is at all likely to be a heavy fall. The labour of having to go over the trees two or three times must not be considered if they are to be saved from injury. It is much better to keep constantly knocking the snow off with light switches, than take the risk of having the trees crushed out of shape and broken.

THE MANAGEMENT AND TRAINING
OF YOUNG TREES

In my last chapter I dealt almost exclusively with the management of old trees. In this chapter I intend to devote the space principally to the treatment that will have to be followed in the training and shaping of young trees in the Topiary garden. I shall try to give as clear and concise an idea as possible to those who are contemplating laying out a garden, or who may already have done so, in which Topiary work is intended to be the main feature, although the training and shaping of young trees does not belong entirely to a garden in course of formation. Generally in old gardens, trees will be found in the course of being trained. If the garden has been laid out and the trees carefully planted on the lines advised in a previous chapter, a record should be carefully made as to the exact date when each tree was planted and also regarding the shape that each tree in the garden is intended to represent when it is finished. A record of that description, made at the period of the work, will prove of great interest in after years, both to those who own the garden and to others who are either interested in it or may happen to visit it. A record of the date of planting and the shapes that the trees were originally meant to represent, seems to have been a thing quite neglected during the formation of the old Topiary gardens, which seems to me to be a very great pity.

Page 36

GUNNERSBURY
AND ASCOTT } Leopold De
Rothchild

Leven Hall

Danesfield – Marlow
Friars Park = Henley on-Thames
Claremont
Compton Wynyate

COMPANY	VISITING		DATE	TIME IN
HEPWORM ENG	D. MITCHALL	P798 JNG	17/4/97	12.10

WELCOME TO

Croudace

EMERGENCY PROCEDURES IF THE ALARM SOUNDS PLEASE FOLLOW THE INSTRUCTIONS OF YOUR HOST.

SMOKING PLEASE OBSERVE THE NO SMOKING POLICY.

HEALTH & SAFETY YOU ARE SUBJECT TO OUR HEALTH & SAFETY REGULATIONS WHICH ARE AVAILABLE ON REQUEST.

THE PASS BADGE MUST BE WORN AT ALL TIMES AND RETURNED TO RECEPTION PRIOR TO LEAVING

To a great extent the general management of young trees is altogether different from the management required to be given to old trees; inasmuch as the difficulties are more numerous, and the care and attention necessary to be bestowed on them more manifold. Our forefathers with the greatest skill and care laid out and formed the old established Topiary gardens of the present day, and afterwards year by year trained and shaped the fine old specimens of the Topiary art now to be seen in some of the old gardens, so that when a person is walking through one of these gardens, and examining the quaint and curious shapes of the trees, he cannot fail to admire them and to reflect upon the amount of skill and labour that has been bestowed on them. It would be curious, indeed, if he failed to pause, and consider the amount of patience the gardeners of earlier years were endowed with. In many respects the gardener of the present time has the advantage in Topiary work at least over his brother of one or two hundred years ago. Whether the gardeners of the present day are more skilled in that special art, is a question which I am not prepared to answer; but I am certain that there is no mistaking the abilities of the old gardeners in the art of training trees. The work they have left behind them proves this beyond a doubt. The gardener of the present day has more variety of shapes to choose from, and a larger and more varied selection of trees to work upon.

If the trees were a good size and well grown when they were planted, the work of clipping and training them may be commenced the following year, according to the shape into which it is intended to form the tree. It is not advisable that any clipping or training be done to the trees the same autumn or winter that they are planted. It should be deferred until the following autumn, in order to allow of fresh root action taking place. Some of the trees can be clipped into certain shapes when they are quite small; but for other shapes a much larger tree is necessary to commence work upon. It is a very wise policy to go to a little extra expense on the original outlay of the trees, rather than buy small trees that will be of no use whatever for the work for which they are ultimately intended.

If the suggestion that I made in a previous chapter has been acted upon, viz., the buying in of the required number of trees some years before the work of making the garden is taken in hand, and bringing them on in the home nursery beds until they have become a suitable size, and until the time arrives when they are required for planting in their permanent places in the garden, the actual cost of the trees will be reduced to a minimum, and better and more suitable trees secured than if they had been purchased direct from some of the nurserymen.

Although no actual shaping need be done to them until they are planted in their places in the garden where they are to remain, a little pruning and regulating of the shoots may be carried out. If that is done, it will be found to be a great advantage in adapting the trees to their future work. The buying of young trees from the nurserymen and growing them on in nursery beds in the reserve garden, until they are required for planting in the garden, is a system regularly practised here, and one that is well worth a trial.

To the person desirous of having a Topiary garden there are two courses open. The first is, he can either train and shape his own trees, or else he can purchase from one or other of the nurserymen who make clipped yews a speciality, a ready-made collection. Trees that are clipped into all manner of shapes can now be purchased from some of the nurserymen either at home

A VERDANT PEACOCK

or imported from the Continent. The system of buying trees that are already shaped is an excellent way of getting a Topiary garden made and furnished with trees in the quickest possible time. But it is a plan that is not to be universally recommended or practised. In the first place, trees of that description generally have the very great drawback of being very expensive. Only those who have to deal with the training of yews have any idea how much labour and care is spent on a tree in shaping it into even the smallest bird; and it therefore stands to reason that the time and labour nurserymen spend on clipping and training Topiary trees, and preparing them for the market, must be paid for by the purchaser. But there is another, and perhaps an even greater objection in buying trees already trained. Surely the person who loves his garden and takes a great personal interest in Topiary work, would never think of planting it with trees that have already been cut into shapes by other hands. Although there is no question about the excellence of nursery trained trees, I would strongly recommend that the person who spends the time and money in forming and laying out a Topiary garden, should have the patience to undertake and carry through the training of his own trees. A far greater source of pleasure will be derived from watching your own trees grow, and from seeing them clipped and trained each year into the particular shape that it is intended they should represent.

It has been very often said, and said with a great deal of truth, that a person can with care and management train the yew into almost any shape desired. Even figures or letters are easy to form out of yew. In handling the yew, you have a kind of tree to work upon that lends itself in the most convenient way to the work of clipping and training into all the quaint and curious shapes that are found in the Topiary gardens. The adaptation of the tree for the work, and the ease with which it can be twisted and bent into almost any conceivable shape, places it far before any other for the particular work I am describing. Therefore no fear need be entertained that there will be any lack of variety of shapes in the garden; provided, of course, that due care is exercised at the commencement of the work, and that each individual tree is clipped and trained to represent an entirely different design or figure, as the case may be. As a matter of fact, in any garden that contains, say, one hundred trees or even more, out of all that number no two trees need be exactly alike. Each can be made to represent an absolutely different shape. Of course there is no reason, except as a matter of taste, why each tree should be made to represent quite a distinct shape from its neighbour. It might be considered a better plan to plant the trees in pairs, side by side, or on the opposite sides of a walk, and then train and shape them into pairs resembling each other in every way. Training in pairs is an arrangement that might find favour with some, and to a certain extent might be adopted with advantage in the garden, especially at the ends of paths. If it is decided to clip some of the trees in pairs resembling each other, they should be those that are planted near the ends of the path, one on each side. If there are two trees planted one on each side of the path, the effect is better if they are clipped into identically the same shape than would be the case if they both represented something different. But I think, on the whole, if there is anything to choose between the two styles, the one tree one shape style should have the preference, if only for the sake of variety.

In the matter of shapes, it is no use trying to lay

SEAT AT THE PRIORY, GLASTONBURY

down a hard and fast rule, as every person who owns, or intends to own, a Topiary garden, will almost to a certainty please himself as to the designs into which he will have his trees shaped. However, I will try to give my readers some little idea of the different shapes it is possible to make out of the yew tree. In the first instance, almost any letter of the alphabet can, with comparative ease, be represented ; and nearly all of them can be done with a single tree, although in the case of some letters, two or even three trees may be required to form the letter as quickly as possible. In the shaping of the letter A, for instance, two trees will be necessary for the purpose. Suppose it is intended to make a capital letter A. In the first place select two well-furnished trees five or six feet in height, and not more than nine inches in diameter at the base, and plant them as already advised, four, five, or even six feet apart, according to the size it is intended to make the letter. One at least of the two trees should have two leading shoots growing from it ; one to be trained straight up to form the inside of the letter, and the other to be trained across to form the middle of the letter. But, if both trees are furnished with two leading shoots, one of each can be trained across to form the cross part of the letter. If two trees can be got, with two leading shoots, as I pointed out, they will equalise the balance of the letter better, and give a more even appearance to the tree. In the case of the letter B, one tree only will be required for the purpose, if the letter is intended to be, say, eight or nine feet high. To be exact, we will suppose it is intended to form the letter B, nine feet high. The tree that is chosen for the purpose should have only one single stem for half of the way up the tree. It should then branch into three leaders or main shoots, as from this point three branches or stems will be required to make up the different portions of the letter.

The strongest or main stem of the tree should be made use of to form the straight side of the letter. Then utilise the two remaining stems in forming the two halves of the B. The one that is growing in the most suitable position for the purpose can be bent round to form the top half ; while the other stem is made to do the same in the case of the bottom part. In very much the same way the letters C, D, E and F can be trained, or even any letter of the alphabet. There is not a single letter from A to Z that it is not possible to train into shape ; some are perhaps more difficult than others to do, but they can all be done, and well done, if they are carefully handled. The principal thing to remember is the selecting of trees that are most suitable for the purpose. Always aim at finding trees with the requisite number of shoots that will be required to form the different parts of the letter it is intended to make. If it is the intention of the Topiarist to form one or more letters of the alphabet, trees for the purpose should if possible be selected some years before being wanted, and should be prepared for the work intended. Trees that are so prepared beforehand will immediately they are planted in the garden be in a fit condition to shape into letters at once. If the trees are treated in this way, it will in a marked degree do away with the necessity of keeping the letters for several years in the garden in the ugly first stages of formation. There must, of course, be always a time when any tree that is being trained looks unsightly to the person who is new to the art of Topiary work. In the training of letters especially, it will be found much safer, and certainly a great deal easier, if iron frameworks are used. This certainly simplifies the work to a great extent. By using a light framework, a more equally proportioned letter can be made than will be the case if the more rough and ready method of using wooden supports be practised. Of course it is quite possible to train almost any letter, and succeed in making a fairly good job of it, with the aid of a little assistance in the shape of a few wooden supports, etc. But wood is never very satisfactory, for this reason—that when it is used, it will have to be in most cases green, in order to make it pliable and easy to bend. Green wood has a tendency to decay very soon, and the first strong winds that come will very likely break the supports, and blow the whole thing to pieces, or at least damage it so as to make it require to be re-trained again. In the process of training yew or any other tree into letters, the appearance of each letter will be greatly improved if from one and a half to two feet of stem be left between the ground and the commencement of the letter. This stem should be afterwards planted round with small boxwood trees, and clipped so as to form a pedestal, which may be of any shape desired. There are two ways or shapes into which letters can be trained, either the round or the square. The square way of training them is the one I would strongly recommend to my readers, from an ornamental point of view, but it is at the same time the most difficult method. As I explained in my last chapter, anything with square edges is more difficult to clip exactly right than a round object.

In the Topiary garden, the variety of shapes that it is possible to train are so many and varied that I will only give a few of those that can either be copied from the old gardens, or formed from the Topiarist's own ideas. In the first instance, there are the various shapes of the figures required in the game of chess. Birds of any description are easy to form into shape in either yew or boxwood. When they are well trained and properly shaped, nothing has a better appearance in the Topiary garden than the various shapes of birds. The shaping of animals is more difficult to manage ; but I have seen some good specimens, notably a lion and crown, the Howard crest, that we have got in the garden here at Levens. Then there are the various other shapes that are to be found in the old Topiary gardens, such as barristers' wigs, Indian wigwams, summer-houses, helmets, busbys, bottles of almost any description or size, umbrellas, hats or spirals of various forms. These may be either trained as single trees, or formed into arches. Among the newer shapes that I have seen, which have recently been introduced into the Topiary art, are yachts, boats, jugs, etc. The different sizes and shapes of jugs are so varied, that any person who fancies the training of them in his garden need not lack variety of form, and they are shapes that are, comparatively speaking, very easy to train. There are also a great many very pretty shapes that can be formed out of the yew or the boxwood tree without being intended to represent anything in particular, further than that they are trained and shaped simply as ornaments to help to add further to the embellishment of the garden.

It is not my intention to try to explain the various ways of training all the different shapes I have pointed out. That in itself would require a chapter ; as the different ways of training a yew or any other tree are so numerous, to attain what is practically the same end, that the person responsible for the work will have to be guided greatly by circumstances and according to the particular tree he has got to work upon. In every Topiary garden there should be at least four or five different arches of various designs. There are very few things that are more effective in any garden than a few well-trained arches, and in the Topiary garden, if they are not more effective than in the modern garden, they are at any rate more in keeping with the general surroundings of the place. If it has been decided to train several arches in the garden, each one should be

LEVENS GARDENS: UMBRELLA, INDIAN WIGWAM AND EAST WALK

quite a different shape from its neighbour. There is such a variety of different shapes to be seen in almost any garden where arches are trained, that there is no occasion for two arches in one garden to be similar in design.

When the shapes have been carefully thought out, let no time be lost in making a start on the clipping and training of them, especially if the trees are far enough advanced in growth to begin work on. It is simply loss of time to allow the trees to keep growing, year after year, when they might be having some training done to advantage towards the clipping and shaping of them. It is a very great mistake to allow young trees to grow for several years after they are large enough to be fit for training. As soon as ever a tree is large enough to begin work on according to the shape the tree is intended to be, a start should be made, or else it will be found when the work is begun, that some branches that have taken three or four years to grow will have to be cut away altogether, after serving no other purpose than exhausting in an unnecessary manner the strength of the tree; whereas if the tree had been clipped sooner, these branches could have been utilised in forming its various parts, or else removed from the tree.

In the making of a Topiary garden, nothing should be done to the trees in a hurry; but on the other hand, no more time should be lost than can possibly be avoided in hastening on the work of shaping, and in getting the garden furnished in the quickest possible time. No young shoots or branches should be cut away that can possibly be used in the construction of the various shapes; but in the training of young trees special care should be given to them, and particular notice taken that they are not allowed to make too rapid growth. In a very few years trees will be injured to a great extent through being allowed to grow too quickly. More especially does this apply to hedges. No matter how much it is desired to get a hedge quickly grown in a certain place, whether for shelter or anything else, it is the greatest possible mistake to sacrifice strength and substance to a desire to promote rapid growth, a result that is certain to occur if a hedge is allowed to grow eight or ten feet before it is stopped. Nothing should be done to a hedge in the way of clipping the same autumn or winter it is planted, and perhaps not even the following autumn; but each year afterwards it should be stopped, and never allowed to make more than three or four inches of growth each year. By following the system of stopping the growth every year, the length of time required to grow a hedge eight or ten feet in height is greatly extended. But the result will amply repay the extra time that has been taken to grow it; you will get a hedge full of strength and substance, and well furnished with young growths from top to bottom. But if the other system is followed of allowing the hedge to get to its full height before any clipping is done, you will have a hedge that is lacking in strength and substance, easily blown out of shape by every wind, and also one that it is very difficult to clip in anything like a proper way, on account of its many strong branches growing towards the outside, that should have been removed to make room for a thicker growth. Each year when the work of clipping is being done, a sharp lookout should be kept for all small branches or shoots that are inclined to grow towards the outside of the tree or hedge, and these must be removed whenever they are seen. In equal force does this apply to both hedges and trees, and it is a part of the work in a Topiary garden which if not carefully attended to, will very soon cause a great deal of harm. Those shoots in the course of a few years will grow into strong branches, and become a regular nuisance in the way of keeping them constantly

ARM-CHAIR IN BOX AT COMPTON WYNYATES

tied in ; and eventually it is possible that they will have to be removed altogether, as it is not always easy to keep branches of that description tied back within the general level of the hedge. Nothing, moreover, gives a worse appearance to a hedge or tree than one of these bare branches projecting beyond the general level, perhaps entirely devoid of young growth. In the case of one of these branches that I have described having been allowed to grow for some years, and then found necessary to be removed by being cut out altogether, the disfigurement that will be caused to the hedge or tree will be very apparent for some years afterwards ; whereas, if such branches had been removed each year as they made their appearance, no disfigurement would have resulted through their removal ; rather would the growth be improved to a great extent, inasmuch as, where each shoot or branch is cut off a number of young growths will break away, which will help to give the hedge a firm and compact appearance, a thing that is greatly to be desired in all clipped hedges or trees. For the general work of clipping and training trees in the Topiary garden, I would strongly recommend that the old-fashioned shears be used. There are several different makes of clipping shears to be got now. Some of them have been given a trial here ; but for general purposes they were not found to be very well suited to the work. There are exceptions, of course, where they might be used with advantage, as, for instance, in the case of a privet hedge, where the surface is smooth and even and the growth soft and easily cut. But for all general purposes, the old style of shears is the best. It is very often the case that in the work of clipping a well trained tree, it is necessary to cut the growths off one by one, and it is in a similar instance that the old-fashioned shears with their sharp points have the advantage over the newer make of machine.

THE GENERAL MANAGEMENT OF A
TOPIARY GARDEN

In previous chapters I have dealt almost entirely with
the general formation of a Topiary garden; the soils
and manures that are most suitable for the cultivation
and welfare of the yew; and I tried to give my readers
some idea of the general treatment required in the
management of both old and young trees.   In this
chapter it is my intention to explain, as clearly as
possible, the yearly management of a Topiary garden.

The general routine of work in the Formal or Dutch
garden is very much the same as in any other garden,
with, of course, the exception of the clipping and training
of the trees.   That in itself adds a very great amount
of extra labour to the general work.   But fortunately it
is work that requires to be done at the slackest time
of the year for gardening, viz., the autumn.

If the garden is an old established one, the arranging
and planting of the different beds will have been carried
out many years previous, very possibly at the time the
trees were planted, at the foundation of the garden,
although there is no doubt they will have been subject
to many alterations during the years that have elapsed
since the time when the garden was first formed.   But
in this chapter it is with the planting and arranging of
the various flowering plants in the beds of a garden
that has been laid out on the principle recommended in
an earlier chapter of this work—on the formation of the
Topiary garden—that I intend chiefly to deal with.

THE COTTAGER'S PRIDE

The planting of the beds and their various contents is in the Topiary garden a very important part of the work, and one that requires both a great amount of skill and forethought, as to a great extent on the arranging of the various kinds of flowering plants in the different beds will depend the future beauty of the garden. Of course I do not mean to imply that the arrangement of the various beds is of as much importance as the planting of the trees, as they differ in this respect so far, that once the trees in a Topiary garden are planted, they should under no circumstances whatever be altered; but in the case of the beds, they may be subject to many alterations, as circumstances may occur. The yew by itself is not a very bright or attractive tree, but when you see it planted in the Topiary garden and clipped into all kinds of unique shapes and figures, and all the available space in the beds is utilised for the purpose of massing either herbaceous or bedding plants, the effect is extremely beautiful; it is then that one sees a garden with a charm and beauty about it that is very seldom if ever met with in the more modern garden.

It is quite evident that, in most of the old formal gardens, glass accommodation has never to any great extent been considered necessary. Yet there is nothing of more importance to the gardener in charge of a large Topiary garden than plenty of glass accommodation for storing the various bedding plants during winter and spring. In former years both the persons who owned the Topiary gardens, and the gardeners as well, seem to have depended to a great extent on the different varieties of annuals for the embellishment of their gardens. But annuals in a garden such as the one I am speaking of, never have the same effect among the yews as the more bright and showy bedding plants. I quite agree with a great many people in their contention that glass structures are altogether out of place in the Topiary garden. But provision should be made for them in some way or other, and as a rule some place can be found for the erection of a few houses without clashing with the other features of the garden.

If the garden has been laid out on a large scale, and contains a quantity of large beds, as regards the work of arranging and deciding what each bed is to be planted with, the person who is responsible will have to be guided by circumstances to a certain extent according to the accommodation that is already at hand, or is to be provided for the raising of bedding plants.

In every garden, and especially in the Topiary garden, the beds should be so arranged that they will yield as far as possible a continual show of bloom for as many months of the year as flowers will bloom in the garden. A continual supply of bloom for the longest possible time is the principal object to be aimed at. Of course in the arrangement of the beds it will be necessary to plant some of them with herbaceous plants; others may be planted with roses; as both roses and herbaceous plants look well in any garden. But in the using of perennial plants of any kind, I would strongly recommend that they should be planted more in the background and in large borders, instead of in the more important beds in the garden. These last should be reserved for bedding plants, as no matter whether roses, or any other kind of plants, be used, the same brilliant and desirable effect can never be obtained as is to be had from the more showy and more easily massed bedding plants. In the planting of herbaceous or any variety of plants, exceptional care should be taken to keep the plants far enough away from the trees, so as to avoid all injurious effects from the summer's growth coming in contact with the yews. If the practice of planting close up to the trees is followed, on purpose to avoid bare patches in

A SWAN CUT IN BOX AT COMPTON WYNYATES

COTTAGE TOPIARY AT NORTH WEALD, ESSEX

the borders, the result will be disastrous to the more important part of the garden, viz., the Topiary work. But as bare patches are always unsightly in the border, they should be avoided as far as possible by planting the very dwarf growing herbaceous plants in close proximity to the trees. It is a plan that can very well be followed in perennial planting, but it is more difficult to manage in the more important work of bedding out for the summer months, especially if large and tall growing plants are extensively used.

If it should happen, as I remarked before in this chapter, that the glass accommodation is limited, it is of particular importance that the utmost use be made of what there is at hand for the storing and propagating of bedding plants, more especially if the requirements of the place are such as to make an autumn display of bloom one of the most important features in the garden. If such is the case, it will be necessary when the bedding season arrives, to be careful that only such plants are used as will be at their best in the autumn, more especially in the most important beds. No attempt whatever should be made at carpet bedding; it is a style of bedding that has very little to recommend it at any time and certainly none in the Topiary garden; for one reason it is much too stiff for a garden where there are a great many clipped yews. Of course in a new garden that has been recently laid out and where both the trees and the box edging are in a small state, the system of carpet bedding may be practised by those who wish to entirely discard Nature from their gardens. But if the garden is an old one, full of old specimen yews, the larger and taller growing the bedding plants are that are used for bedding out purposes, the better. I will name a few of the bedding plants that are extensively used in the gardens here at Levens; but of course, as is well known, the gardens here are among the oldest

examples of Topiary work in England. There are some
varieties of bedding plants that are far more effective
than others when planted among yews, and among the
most suitable, there is nothing that has more effect than
the brilliant scarlet Lobelia cardinalis and its varieties.
Some objection may perhaps be taken to the plant by
some people, but when planted in large masses among
the sombre yews in a Topiary garden, I have not the
slightest hesitation in saying it has no equal : when
growing in large masses with a background of green
yew and the sun shining on the dark foliage and brilliant
scarlet flowers, the effect is really beautiful. Perhaps
the only drawback to the various varieties of Lobelia
cardinalis is the difficulty experienced by some in keeping
it over winter ; but if instead of following the old system
of partly drying it off in winter, directly it is lifted out of
the beds, one places it in a frame or greenhouse with a
gentle heat and gives it a fair amount of water, thus
encouraging it to start into growth at once, the difficulty
will to a very great extent be done away with. Another
favourite plant here, and one that is greatly used for
bedding out purposes in the Topiary garden, is the
beautiful old-fashioned plant Salvia patens. Like the
scarlet lobelias, Salvia patens should be largely grown in
every garden where there are a lot of yews. The
brilliant blue of the flowers against the dark green of
the yew trees has a very striking effect indeed, either
when planted in masses by itself or mixed in the beds
along with the scarlet lobelia or the tall yellow
Calceolarias amplexicaulis. But the foliage of the Salvia
patens has not the same showy appearance as that of the
Lobelia cardinalis, but this is a point that can be over-
looked, as the brilliant blue of the flowers fully com-
pensates one for the lack of beauty in the plant, and it
rarely happens among the general stock of bedding
plants that one can find plants with foliage and flowers

equally effective. But in my opinion, if a fault is to be found with the Salvia patens as a bedding plant, it is its inability to withstand wet weather. Through that cause it is very often denuded of its flowers, but it very soon revives with a few bright days. Among other plants that are extremely useful for bedding purposes in the Topiary garden are the taller growing varieties of fuschias that are hardy enough to stand planting out in the flower garden, and more especially if the yews are old and large ; fuschias planted either in clumps or massed alone in large beds with a groundwork of violas, or some other suitable plants, will give a very striking effect among yews, and they have the additional advantage of giving a good show of bloom during a mild autumn long after the majority of bedding plants have finished flowering, which is a quality that ought to recommend them in any garden as well as the Topiary one. In most gardens, variety of plants is considered a necessity in the work of bedding out, and space will not permit me to point out the special qualities of each and every different variety of plant that may be used in the embellishment of a Topiary garden, but I will give the names of a few that I have found most suitable and effective for bedding out in a garden where the yew tree is extensively grown. The different types of antirrhinums, both dwarf and tall growing varieties, calceolarias, cannas, begonias, heliotropes, yellow and white marguerites, gladioli, and the various varieties of geraniums. Geraniums, and more especially the ivy leaved varieties, should be given a place in the garden if beds that are suitable for them blooming well can be found for them. Grown as pyramids or trained over a wire framework three or four feet high, the effect is very pretty.

In all the bedding arrangements of a Topiary garden, a natural appearance is a thing that should be studied and as much as possible sought. Always remember that in the practice of clipping and training yews into all kinds of shapes, Nature is to a very great extent discarded, therefore there is all the more reason why it should be as much as possible encouraged among the plants in the flower garden; all stiffness should be avoided and as little tying as possible done; though of course a certain amount of tying will be necessary to keep the wind and storm from breaking the plants, unless, indeed, the garden is a sheltered one.

There is another point that should be aimed at in the old formal garden, and that is, to always keep the garden well supplied with old-fashioned flowers. I certainly do not mean it to be understood that none of the new and beautiful varieties of the different species of garden plants that are being introduced every year should not be given a place in the garden, but what I want to be understood is this, that there should not be a wholesale clearing out of the old favourites to make room for the new ones.

As I pointed out before, the general routine of work in the Topiary garden is, with the exception of the clipping and training part of the work, practically the same as in any other garden. If there is a kitchen garden, a necessity that almost every garden, whether Topiary or otherwise, is almost certain to have attached to it, the work of looking after and attending to the various kinds of vegetables will have to be seen to, and a trim and tidy appearance kept in it, more especially if it is combined with the Topiary garden.

If the garden has been laid out on the principle recommended in the chapter dealing with the Formation of a Topiary Garden, and the paths in the flower garden and grounds are composed principally of grass, a fair amount of care and attention will have to be given to them to keep them in proper order. Grass paths are,

LEVENS GARDENS: SHOWING LETTER B AND LION

and always have been, one of the principal features of the formal garden, and no amount of labour and care should be considered wasted in keeping them in good condition. Grass paths require far more labour and attention in keeping them in proper order than those that are composed of some hard substratum, especially if there is a considerable amount of traffic on them; if such is the case, it will be necessary to go over them every spring and re-turf places that have got worn out, afterwards well rolling them; then during the summer and autumn months they will require constant attention in the way of mowing and in keeping the edges well clipped so as to maintain a clean and tidy appearance.

In the Topiary garden it should always be remembered that everything should be kept in as trim and formal a condition as possible, with the exception of the different varieties of plants or shrubs that have been planted for the purpose of giving colour to the garden; amongst those, Nature should as far as is consistent be encouraged; but the walks, beds and borders, and everything else in the garden should be made to present as formal an appearance as possible. If the garden is a formal one, let as much as possible in it be made to have a formal appearance.

In writing on the Topiary garden, I have perhaps made it appear to some of those who may read it as hideously unnatural, and I am aware there are plenty who maintain that it is a style of gardening that has nothing to recommend or encourage about it. But those who think that the formal garden is without its charm make a very great mistake, as in every old world garden there is a charm that belongs to it only. In the woods and the parks let us by all means study and cultivate Nature as far as possible; but in the gardens we should have the trees to present as neat and formal an appearance

as possible, a thing that can only be had by the aid
of constant clipping or pruning.

For a great many years past, in this country at
least, the Topiary garden has been to a very large
extent a thing that belongs to other ages; especially
does this apply to the formation of new gardens; but
there is not wanting evidence at the present day that
it is again coming into favour, and deservedly so. The
Topiary garden has its drawbacks, principally on account
of the great number of years it takes to bring it to
perfection and the amount of extra labour that requires
to be spent over the clipping at various periods of
the year. There is one thing to remember about the
Topiary garden, it is all work.

Perhaps at the present time Topiary gardening is a
subject of far greater interest to rich men in America
than it is over here, and as gardening might practically
be said to be in its infancy in that great country, there
is hardly any reason why the art of Topiary work may
not have a great future in store for it in America.

INDEX

79